Wildflowers

OF THE BLUE RIDGE AND GREAT SMOKY MOUNTAINS

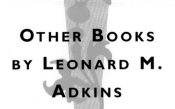

OTHER BOOKS BY LEONARD M. ADKINS

Wildflowers of the Appalachian Trail (Joe and Monica Cook, photographers)

The Appalachian Trail: A Visitor's Companion

Walking the Blue Ridge: A Guide to the Trails of the Blue Ridge Parkway

Best of the Appalachian Trail: Day Hikes (with Victoria and Frank Logue)

Best of the Appalachian Trail: Overnight Hikes (with Victoria and Frank Logue)

50 Hikes in Northern Virginia: Walks, Hikes, and Backpacks from the Allegheny Mountains to the Chesapeake Bay

50 Hikes in Southern Virginia: Walks, Hikes, and Backpacks from the Cumberland Gap to the Atlantic Ocean

50 Hikes in Maryland: Walks, Hikes, and Backpacks from the Allegheny Plateau to the Atlantic Ocean

50 Hikes in West Virginia: Walks, Hikes, and Backpacks from the Allegheny Mountains to the Ohio River

Maryland: An Explorer's Guide

Seashore State Park: A Walking Guide

Adventure Guide to Virginia

The Caribbean: A Walking and Hiking Guide

Wildflowers

OF THE BLUE RIDGE AND GREAT SMOKY MOUNTAINS

authored by **Leonard M. Adkins**

photographed by **Joe Cook**

Menasha Ridge Press
Birmingham, AL

Published by Menasha Ridge Press

Distributed by The Globe Pequot Press

Printed in China

Library of Congress Cataloging-in-Publication Data

Adkins, Leonard M.

Wildflowers of the Blue Ridge and Great Smoky Mountains/ by Leonard M. Adkins; photographs by Joe Cook.

p. cm.

Includes bibliographical references and index.

ISBN 0-89732-567-2

1. Wild flowers—Blue Ridge Mountains—Identification. 2. Wild flowers—Great Smoky Mountains (N.C. and Tenn.)—Identification. I. Cook, Joe, 1966– II. Title.

QK122.3.A452 2005

582.13'09755—dc22   2004059540

Cover and text design by Grant M. Tatum

Photographs by Joe Cook

Menasha Ridge Press

P. O. Box 43673

Birmingham, AL 35243

www.menasharidge.com

TABLE OF CONTENTS

DEDICATION

In memory of my mother, Nancy Adkins. The elegance of the wildflowers pale in comparison to the beauty of the life she lived.

Tom Wieboldt, senior laboratory specialist with the Virginia Tech Herbarium, and Henning Von Schmelling, horticulturist with the Chattahoochee Nature Center, went through and referenced more than 120 photographs to verify the genus and species of each flower. (If there are any errors or omissions of information, the responsibility is ours, and not theirs.)

~ *Leonard and Joe*

Many individuals assisted me with locating and photographing the wildflowers for this book. Foremost among them was Henning Von Schmelling. My top assistant was my daughter, Ramsey Cook, whose keen eyes helped me locate many a flower and whose patience was tried many a time as she held light reflectors and plastic tarps for my shoots. Elizabeth Turner, Tillie Carter, Karen Mickler, Dave Goldman, Carol Weeks, and Robert and Karen Rankin also pitched in with a helping hand or a place to stay during my travels. Thanks!

~ *Joe*

Joe—Once again you have done a fantastic job. Thanks for having the patience to devote two full years to traveling, hiking, and photographing.

Dr. Stephen Lewis, Caroline Charonko, Susie Surfas, and Terry Cumming—Flowers come, flowers go, and I am still here to experience it all because of you.

Kathleen, John, Tim, and Jay Yelenic—Your support is now more important to me than ever.

Ann B. Messick—Thank you for sharing your love and knowledge of the wildflowers with me.

Laurie—Unlike the wildflowers that appear and fade with the seasons, my love for you grows with each passing year.

~ *Leonard*

ACKNOWLEDGMENTS

A woodland walk, a quest for river grapes, a mocking thrush, a wild rose, or a rock-living columbine, salve my worst wounds.

~ *Ralph Waldo Emerson*

Wildflowers. There are few things in this world that can give us so much pleasure and beauty while requiring us to put forth so little effort. Great art can take years to create, and you may have to travel hundreds or thousands of miles to see it. Chefs may spend hours preparing a wonderfully presented meal, yet it might disappoint the taste buds.

It can take effort to observe birds or wildlife. You may need to purchase binoculars, journey to a specific site, be quiet and patient and, then, if you are lucky, you may get a brief glimpse of an animal or bird before it dashes into the undergrowth or takes wing toward the horizon.

However, you don't have to spend any money on special equipment nor must you travel to an exotic location to enjoy the wildflowers—and they are always firmly rooted and won't go scampering off when you approach. Just a short, easy walk in your local woods or park, or down the street where you live will reveal scores of flowers in a wondrous variety of sizes, shapes, and colors. If you don't feel like walking, you can see dozens of blossoms on a leisurely drive down a country lane or, for that matter, even while zipping down an interstate. For some of us, appreciating the wildflowers can involve nothing more than lounging on the living room couch and looking out the window into the front yard.

Those of us who visit or live in the Blue Ridge and Great Smoky Mountains are especially blessed. For almost nowhere else in the world are there the lushness and variety of trees, flowers, shrubs, and other plants as in these mountains. In the Great Smokies alone, there are more species growing than in all of Europe. Only in the South American rain forests is it possible to find a larger variety of plants per acre than those that occur in the Blue Ridge Mountains.

Beyond just admiring their beauty, one of the best ways to appreciate the wildflowers is to learn something about

INTRODUCTION

them. How did they come by their common and scientific names? Why does one flower grow in bottomlands, while another is only found on lofty heights? What caused a plant to evolve into the shape we see today, and what birds and animals are attracted to it? What role has each plant played throughout history, and what has been its value in folkloric as well as modern medicine?

Upon learning all these things, you will find that the greatest lesson is that all things in life are interrelated: what affects one thing affects all things, including humankind. Knowing this will instill a respect and love for the wonderful natural world that we have inherited, and an understanding of why we must work hard to protect and conserve what we will pass on to future generations. It was in this spirit that *Wildflowers of the Blue Ridge and Great Smoky Mountains* was written and photographed. Go forth, see what there is to see, and learn what there is to learn. *Happy wildflowering.*

~ Leonard M. Adkins

A SHORT HISTORY OF THE BLUE RIDGE AND GREAT SMOKY MOUNTAINS

At various times through the ages, the area now known as the Blue Ridge Mountains, stretching from northern Georgia to central Pennsylvania, has risen to great heights from the sea or has sunk to become the floor of a vast ancient ocean. For millions of years, like the rest of the North American continent, the land has been alternately subjected to the effects of movements of the earth's crustal plates, rising and falling seas, erosion from wind and water, and advancing and receding glaciers.

Each time the crustal plates collided, North America assumed a new face. Giant land masses grinding into each other caused the earth's surface to break, crack, and fold upward, creating mountains. At the same time, large slabs of the lower portions of the crust slid underneath one another, raising the surface even higher.

About 200 million years ago, the plates began to split and drift apart, creating the Atlantic Ocean. Several theories maintain that, at one time, the Blue Ridge may have been as rugged and tall as the present-day Rocky Mountains. Erosion by wind and rain has been wearing away these heights bit by bit. Some of the sand that children use to build a sand castle on Virginia Beach may have once been part of a rock outcropping on the crest of the Blue Ridge Mountains.

Although they did not reach this far south, glaciers have also played an important role in the creation of the present-day landscape. As the great sheets of ice advanced from the north, they forced many plants to "migrate" southward. The Ice Age's cooler temperatures allowed northern vegetation such as Birch, Beech, Fir, and Spruce to begin to compete with, and gain a foothold against, the traditional southern hardwoods of Oak, Poplar, and Hickory. Once the glaciers began to recede and warmer air returned, many of the northern plants died out, unable to tolerate a southern climate. However, the cool temperatures of the higher peaks and ridgelines of the Blue Ridge have allowed some of these plants to remain and prosper, cut off from their relatives several hundred miles to the north.

The southern terminus of the Blue Ridge Mountains is in northern Georgia, but almost immediately the chain splits into. The eastern arm swings out toward the flatter lands of Georgia, North Carolina, and Virginia to form the western boundary of the Piedmont. The western arm, generally at a higher elevation than the eastern prong, is known variously as the Cohutta, Ellijay, Frog, Unicoi, Unaka, Iron, Stone, and Great Smoky Mountains.

Within a day-and-a-half drive of more than fifty percent of America's population, the Great Smoky Mountains

National Park receives more than nine million visits a year, making it the most popular of any national park. Surviving this onslaught are its 1,570 species of flowering plants, more than 200 species of birds, 48 freshwater fishes, 60 mammals, and 2,000 different fungi. Included among the park's 78 kinds of amphibians and reptiles are more than 25 salamander species, giving it the distinction of having the greatest diversity of salamanders in the world.

So much of this disparate life owes it existence to the height of this grand mountain range referred to by Arnold Guyot, a mapmaker and explorer of the 1800s, as "the master chain." The elevation creates what is known as the "orographic effect," which basically means that the mountains make their own weather. For instance, Gatlinburg, Tennessee, which sits on the western boundary of the park, receives an annual rainfall of approximately fifty inches. Yet, in the heart of the Smokies, Clingmans Dome, which is about 5,000 feet higher, sees more than eighty inches of precipitation, much of it in the form of snow and ice.

Where plants grow, and what communities they form, can be directly attributed to the temperatures and moisture found at various elevations. A forest of Spruce and Fir, more typically found in New England and Canada, grows in the Smokies at elevations above 4,500 feet. Adjoining these trees near the summits of the mountains are the northern hardwoods such as American Beech and Yellow Birch, more common to Michigan than the southern Appalachians. The stands found in the Smokies are the highest broad-leaved forests in the eastern part of America. Bluets, Violets, Trilliums, and Trout Lilies cover the forest floor.

Below 4,500 feet, tall and mighty Eastern Hemlocks provide such deep shade that the air underneath their canopy can be ten to twelve degrees cooler than that of the surrounding woods. These venerable giants are reminders that more than 100,000 acres of these mountains have never been timbered, which means that the Smokies embrace the largest expanse of virgin forest east of the Mississippi River.

Black and Scarlet Oaks, and White, Pitch, and Shortleaf Pine dominate below 3,000 feet on the drier southern slopes of the mountains. Included in this forest will also be Yellow Poplar, Dogwood, Hickory, and thickets of Rhododendron and Mountain Laurel.

Covering sheltered slopes and extending into low-elevation coves and valleys, the southern Appalachians' famous cove hardwood forests are encountered at elevations of approximately 4,000 feet and lower. Here is the most diverse forest of all. While other trees can be present, some of the most prevalent are Hickory, Beech, Basswood, Poplar, Sugar Maple, Yellow Birch, Buckeye, Magnolia, Carolina Silverbell, Eastern Hemlock, and White Ash. Before the leafy canopy blocks out most of the sunlight in midspring, the floor of this forest will be dotted with luxuriant growths of Trilliums, Fringed Phacelia, Bloodroot, Hepatica, Rue Anemone, Squirrel Corn, Solomon's Seal, Bellwort, and Lady's Slippers.

Forming a large oval, the two arms of the Blue Ridge come back together near the Roanoke River in Virginia. A number of ranges stretch from east to west between the two main ridges, creating a patchwork of additional high mountain country. Known as the Black, Balsam, Cheoah, Nantahala, and other mountains, these transverse ranges contain mountains that are actually higher than the main backbone of the Blue Ridge. North of the Roanoke River, the Blue Ridge Mountains are basically one narrow ridgeline upon which the Blue Ridge Parkway, Skyline Drive, and Shenandoah National Park are located.

Several miles down the West Virginia–Virginia border, the Blue Ridge enters Maryland on the crest of South

Mountain. Following this ridgeline into the southern portion of Pennsylvania, the mighty mountain range finally comes to an end when it drops into the Cumberland Valley near Carlisle, Pennsylvania.

Within the Blue Ridge and Great Smoky Mountains are lofty ridgelines, hidden hillside coves, river valleys dotted with farmlands, and an abundance of small communities and large cities. This variety of latitudes, elevations, and settings means that you have the opportunity to discover a beauty that comes from the grand diversity of flowers here.

The hardest thing in putting this book together was deciding which of the many wildflowers to include and which to exclude. We began with an inventory of more than 250 species found throughout the region. Dropped from the list were a number of species that were related and quite similar to each other, while we retained a few species that we felt were so common that they needed to be included. A couple of species that are quite rare, and therefore of great interest, were also included, in case you are lucky to come across one or two. The result is a volume composed of more than 130 photographs with detailed descriptions and background information on 120 species. There are also citations of more than 100 additional species that describe their distinguishing features.

To help you understand why certain flowers are missing from this book, we want to let you know that a decision was reluctantly made not to include photographs or descriptions of several species that have recently come under intense pressure from poachers. So as not to aid these reprehensible persons in identifying them, we excluded Goldenseal, Ginseng, and Black Cohosh, among other valuable species.

6

There are also several species that are included in the book, but because of poaching we elected not to give specific sites where you might encounter them. It is our hope that this will help the survival of these flowers, such as Bloodroot, Galax, Lady's Slippers, and Sundew, throughout the region.

As you use this book, please take this admonishment to heart—do not pick, dig, harvest, or disturb any flowers you find! Such activities are illegal in many places and, more importantly, the natural world is having a hard enough time coping with the changes that modern civilization has brought to the planet. Leave the plants where they are so that they may propagate themselves and live out their lives in their native surroundings.

The flowers are arranged in five groups according to flower color: white, yellow to orange, pink to red, violet to blue, and green to brown. If a flower has more than one color, such as Dutchman's-Breeches (white with yellow tips), it is placed within the grouping of its predominant color. A flower that may grow in different colors (Catesby's Trillium may have either white or pink petals) is categorized under the color of which its blossoms are most commonly found (and mention is made of the variant colors).

The plants are arranged within each color group in the order of the time of flowering. So, a flower that appears in March is listed before one that blooms in April. If two plants bloom in the same month but one stops blooming earlier, the short-blooming one is listed first.

Many wildflowers have more than one common name, and some names may not be recognized in various parts of the region. For example, Trout Lily is variously known as Dogtooth Violet, Adder's Tongue, and Fawn Lily. I have used what I believe to be its most widely used name. Other common names are cited within the body of the text, but it is entirely possible that your own research may lead you to discover additional ones.

This confusion of common names was the impetus for Swedish botanist Carl Linnaeus to establish a scientific system of names in the 1700s. Using Latin and Greek words as a base, he identified plants and animals with a genus name (always capitalized) followed by a species name (in lowercase). Thus, no matter how the Trout Lily was known locally, it could be referred to worldwide as *Erythronium americanum*.

For the most part this works well, but you will sometimes find that scientific names do not always agree in various reference books. Scholars have long held to the rule that the first published name of a plant (accompanied by a well-founded description) becomes its scientific name. However, further research into a plant's true characteristics often requires a change in the name, and that name change is noted in the text of this book.

The FLOWER section provides a succinct description of the plant's blossom, giving a general overview of its size, color, shape, and other distinguishing characteristics.

A description of the plant's leaves and average height is found in the LEAVES AND STEM section.

The BLOOM SEASON gives the earliest and latest dates when you may find the plant in bloom. The wide variety of habitats and elevations makes it hard to say exactly when you will find a certain flower in bloom in a certain place. In other words, "March to June" might mean that the blooms appearing on a plant in March in lower elevations or in the southern part of its range might have disappeared by the time the same species blossoms in June along the northern portion of the Blue Ridge Mountains or on the higher elevations.

Because guides that just identify a flower tend to be dry and boring, interesting tidbits about the flower—such as how it reproduces or survives, its reputed medicinal uses, folklore about how it received its name, or data on related species—have been included.

To make things as easy as possible to understand, I have, for the most part, avoided using scientific terms, such as sessile or pinnate, to describe the way a plant looks, opting instead to use the language that all of us employ everyday. However, in order to get you used to using them so that you may understand what is being discussed when you consult other sources, I have included them in several descriptions, and the glossary will define them for you.

One of this book's most distinctive features is that it identifies several places where you may encounter each flower. Bear in mind that the word is *may*—there's no guarantee. Many factors, such as wind, amount of precipitation, temperature, or disturbances to its environment, go into determining how profusely—if at all—a plant may bloom or if it will continue to grow in the same place.

You may find many of the flowers growing along roads in the Blue Ridge and Great Smoky Mountains, and the text will identify highways as specifically as possible. There are references to roads in the Great Smoky Mountains National Park (GSMNP), and milepost points along Skyline Drive in Shenandoah National Park (SNP). Milepost points on the Blue Ridge Parkway (BRP) identify places where the flowers grow next to the road or on trails emanating from that point. Other roads will be identified by name (for example, Foothills Parkway) or highway number (for example, NC 26, I-81, US 50). Again, to be as specific as possible, the citation will provide the county (for example, Botetourt County, Virginia) or cities (for example, between Brevard and Asheville, North Carolina) where the roadway is located.

When a trail is mentioned as being in a certain county (for example, Henry Lanum Trail in Nelson County, Virginia), you will know that it is a forest service trail. Non-forest service trails are cited as being in a specific park or close to a city (for example, House Mountain Trail near Lexington, Virginia). State parks should be easily located on state highway maps. Sites on the Appalachian Trail (for example, on the AT on Max Patch in North Carolina) can be found in the index of their respective Appalachian Trail guides available from the Appalachian Trail Conference, P. O. Box 807, Harpers Ferry, West Virginia 25425, (304) 535-6331; www.atconf.org. Guides for trails in GSMNP may be obtained from Great Smoky Mountains Association, 115 Park Headquarters Road, Gatlinburg, Tennessee 37738, (888) 898-9102; www.smokiesstore.org.

Information on many of the other trails may be found by consulting one or more of my other books, including *Walking the Blue Ridge: A Guide to the Trails of the Blue Ridge Parkway; 50 Hikes in Northern Virginia; 50 Hikes in Southern Virginia;* and *50 Hikes in Maryland.*

You may also note that, to include as many flower sites as possible, I have been somewhat liberal in taking a broader area than geographers would strictly define as the Blue Ridge and Great Smoky Mountains, including some sites that are just a few miles east of the Blue Ridge, some within and along the western edge of the Shenandoah Valley, and even a few on the Allegheny Plateau in Maryland.

Joe and I feel the need to reiterate and reinforce what was said earlier: once you have located the flowers in the field, please do not pick, dig, harvest, or disturb any of them. Several flowers are rare or endangered and are becoming more so with each passing day.

If you are interested in growing wildflowers, you can obtain a list of businesses that propagate them from seeds and cuttings grown in nurseries—contact the North Carolina Botanical Gardens, University of North Carolina, Totten Center, Chapel Hill, NC 27599-3375; www.ncbg.unc.edu.

Wildflowers

RUE ANEMONE

Thalictrum thalictroides

FLOWER:
With one to three blossoms rising from the main stem, the one-inch-wide flowers have five to ten white to pinkish sepals.

LEAVES AND STEM:
A pair, or sometimes a whorl, of one-inch ovate leaves are divided into three lobes and situated below the blossom. A set of basal leaves usually appears on the four- to eight-inch-high stem once the plant has stopped blooming.

BLOOM SEASON:
March to May

Favoring the same rich woodlands as Bloodroot (*Sanguinaria canadensis;* see page 14), the delicate blossoms of Rue Anemone start to appear several weeks before the Wood Anemone (*Anemone quinquefolia;* see page 24), another member of the Buttercup family (which has about 1,100 species worldwide), near which it grows and with which it may be confused. Both plants have flowers with white sepals (there are no petals) that may be tinged with pink. The Rue Anemone's three-lobed leaves are quite distinct from the Wood Anemone's deeply toothed leaves, which may be divided into three to five leaflets. Early Meadow Rue (*Thalictrum dioicum*) has leaves that resemble those of Rue Anemone, but its greenish-white flowers grow in drooping clusters.

For such a lovely flower, Rue Anemone has had a bad reputation through the centuries. People living in northern Africa called it a symbol of illness, and the Chinese a flower of death; Europeans feared it so much that they avoided breathing its scent. All these cultures may have been right, as scientists have discovered that the plant is poisonous.

When looking to other sources for information on Rue Anemone, you should be aware that some reference books still follow an older classification of the plant that was assigned when it was considered a monotypic plant—meaning a species with a genus all to itself—and named *Anemonella thalictroides.*

Some places you may encounter Rue Anemone include: Bradley Fork and Cove Hardwood Nature Trails in GSMNP; on the AT on Max Patch Mountain in North Carolina, Humpback Mountain in central Virginia, and throughout SNP; in Ivy Creek Natural Area near Charlottesville, and along the trails of Sky Meadows State Park in Virginia; and in the upland woods of Catoctin Mountain Park in Maryland.

BLOODROOT

Sanguinaria canadensis

One of the pleasures of a late winter or early spring walk in the woods is spying the tightly wound green leaf of a Bloodroot plant pushing its way through the frost-encrusted soil. When the snowy-white flower rises above the still-furled leaf a day or two later, you know warmer temperatures are on the way.

Each blossom may last for a week or two (if not mangled by heavy rains or high winds), but the distinctive leaf continues to dot the forest floor well into summer, sometimes attaining a breadth of nine inches on a stem that may reach a foot in height. The flower develops into a capsule whose seeds ripen before falling to the ground. The brown seeds are round and may roll several feet from the parent plant, thereby enabling the Bloodroot to extend its range.

The plant's name comes from the red or orange sap that flows freely whenever its stem or root is cut or broken. Native Americans used the liquid as an insect repellent, a treatment for rheumatism and ringworm, and a dye for clothing, baskets, and facial paint. Today, several companies market toothpaste and mouthwash that incorporate ingredients from the plant to help fight plaque buildup and gingivitis, or gum disease. Several studies bear out this claim, but some have shown that it is effective only when both the toothpaste and the mouthwash are used.

Sadly, unscrupulous persons illegally harvest tens of thousands of plants every year for their commercial value. Because of this problem, and in the hope that the plant will continue to be found throughout the region, it was decided not to include in this book specific sites where you might encounter Bloodroot in the Blue Ridge and Great Smoky Mountains.

SERVICEBERRY
Amelanchier canadensis

FLOWER:
The one-inch-wide flowers grow in terminal clusters. Usually appearing on the plant before the leaves do, each star-shaped blossom has five narrow, nearly pure-white petals.

LEAVES AND STEM:
The oblong leaves are a little more than two inches long and about one inch wide. They are sharply toothed, smooth above, and nearly smooth underneath.

BLOOM SEASON:
April to May

Early springtime drives on an otherwise dull and monotonous four-lane highway can be transformed into wondrous trips past hillsides covered with splashes of white Serviceberry flowers. Within a week or two, the clusters are accentuated by the rich purple blossoms covering nearly every inch of neighboring Redbud (*Cercis canadensis;* see page 156) trees. Some people may say that, strictly speaking, trees and shrubs should not be included in a guide to wildflowers.

However, trees are not a group of plants related to each other, but are related to other types of plants. Serviceberry, Apple, Cherry, and Hawthorn trees are Roses, and Redbud and Black Locust are members of the Pea family, which also includes Goat's Rue (*Tephrosia virginiana;* see page 178). Further examples are the Tulip trees and Magnolias, which are related to Buttercups and Anemones. Hackberry and the Elms' links are to Nettles and Marijuana, while the Buckeyes, Hollies, and Maples are closely related to Spotted Jewelweed (*Impatiens capensis;* see page 252) and Poison Ivy.

The Serviceberry tree is a thing of beauty throughout the year. The emerging leaves are a silvery green; after the flower petals have fallen away they turn a full green, helping highlight the reddish-purple berries. As temperatures cool, the foliage adds its own hues of yellow and gold to the forest, while the light gray bark shines in the rays of a winter sun.

Other names for Serviceberry are Sarvisberry, Shadbush, Juneberry, and Shadblow.

Some places you may encounter Serviceberry include: Little River Gorge in GSMNP; BRP mileposts 241–242, 294–297, 308.3, 347.6, and 368–370; on the AT between Indian Gap and Newfound Gap in GSMNP, and between VA 311 and McAfee Knob, and south of Rocky Row Run in central Virginia; Patterson Mountain Trail in Botetourt County, Virginia; and on the Green Ridge Hiking Trail in Allegany County, Maryland.

16

DUTCHMAN'S-BREECHES

Dicentra cucullaria

Looking like freshly laundered and starched pants that have been hung out on the clothesline to dry, the blossoms of the Dutchman's-Breeches sway back and forth in response to the slightest of breezes. Favoring the rich soil of north slopes, they may often be seen growing close to Trout Lily (*Erythronium americanum;* see page 104) and Spring Beauty (*Claytonia virginica;* see page 152). Each Dutchman's-Breeches flower lasts just a few days, and it stops blossoming once the forest canopy blocks the full sunlight. In fact, by midsummer even the plant's leaves will have disappeared, and it may be hard to find any trace that it ever existed.

The shape of the flower easily explains the common name, but its structure also gave rise to its scientific name. Because it is similar in appearance to its relatives Wild Bleeding Heart (*Dicentra eximia;* see page 160) and Squirrel Corn (*Dicentra canadensis;* see page 22), Linnaeus dubbed the genus *Dielytra* for the resemblance to insect wing cases (*ely-trae*). The name was later changed to *Dicentra,* the Greek word for "double-spurred." The species name *cucullaria* means "hooded."

Dutchman's-Breeches were once popular in wild-flower gardens, but numerous authorities have cautioned parents of small children to refrain from including it. The plant is poisonous, containing several isoquinoline alkaloids, including aporphine and protopine, the latter of which is also found in opium poppies.

Some places you may encounter Dutchman's-Breeches include: Cove Hardwood Nature Trail and Balsam Mountain Road in GSMNP; BRP mileposts 359.9, 367.6, and 458.2; on the AT on Bluff Mountain on the North Carolina–Tennessee border, the north slope of Pearis Mountain in southwest Virginia, south of Cow Camp Gap in central Virginia, and in low areas of SNP; and, although not exceedingly common, in the lowlands of Catoctin Mountain Park in Maryland.

WHITE BANEBERRY

Actaea pachypoda

Have midsummer to early fall walks in the woods ever made you feel you were being watched? Well, maybe it wasn't so much "someone" as "something" that was looking at you. At that time of year, the White Baneberry's flowers have developed into its fruits, the porcelain-white berries with a dark purple-to-black dot on them that resemble just exactly what one common name for the plant calls them—Doll's Eyes.

The eyes may have made you feel paranoid, but don't seek revenge by picking and eating them, as they are poisonous. Although robins, wood thrushes, catbirds, thrashers, grouse, and other birds may feast upon them with no ill effect, human adults have experienced dizziness, confusion, difficulty in swallowing, and intense stomach discomfort, and there have been reports of small children dying after ingesting just a few of the berries. In fact, you should avoid the entire plant, as the foliage has been known to produce a skin rash.

Nevertheless, do not overlook the delicate beauty of the White Baneberry's tiny blossoms. The petals and sepals fall away as the flower opens, leaving a feathery-looking mass of yellow-tipped stamens and a single pistil. Because they produce only pollen (and no nectar), the flowers do not attract honeybees but, instead, what biologists call "halictid bees"—those tiny, buzzing harassers, the sweat bees.

When consulting other sources for information on White Baneberry, you should be aware that some reference books list it as *Actaea alba*. Other common names include White Cohosh, Grapewort, Whiteheads, and Necklace Weed.

Some places you may encounter White Baneberry include: Porters Creek, Roaring Fork Motor Nature, Kanati Fork, and Sugarlands Nature Trails in GSMNP; and on the AT between Wayah Gap and Siler Bald in North Carolina.

SQUIRREL CORN

Dicentra canadensis

FLOWER:
The flower is similar to that of
Dutchman's-Breeches, but the upper
spurs are more rounded and point
upward instead of flaring out to the
side, giving it more of a heart shape
than a V, and the lower tip is tinged
purplish-pink rather than yellow.

LEAVES AND STEM:
The leaves are basically like those
of the Dutchman's-Breeches, being
three to six inches long, compound,
and paler underneath.

BLOOM SEASON:
April to May

Similar in appearance to its relatives the Dutchman's-Breeches (*Dicentra cucullaria;* see page 18) and Wild Bleeding Heart (*Dicentra eximia;* see page 160), Squirrel Corn favors the same rich woodland environment and is most often found on rocky northern slopes. Like other members of the genus, it contains toxins that have been known to cause grazing cattle to become ill and sometimes die. Yet, folklore holds that squirrels (and wild turkeys) can feed upon the yellow tubers that grow on its roots—and resemble kernels of corn—without any repercussions.

With a fragrance that reminds some people of Hyacinths, the flower attracts bumblebees, honeybees, and other insects. Only the bumblebee has a tongue long enough to reach the nectar hidden at the far end of the spur, but look closely at the spurs and you may see tiny holes in the tips. Insects whose tongues are too short or whose bodies too large to gain access to the nectar by crawling into the spurs have learned that all they have to do to enjoy the flower's sweet juices is nip the tip.

The flower develops into a long pod with a slender end that opens lengthwise and contains a number of small seeds. These seeds resemble small corn kernels, but their outsides shine like black polished patent leather.

Some places you may encounter Squirrel Corn include: Cove Hardwood Nature Trail, in Chimneys Picnic Area, and Little River and Heintooga Ridge Roads in GSMNP; BRP milepost 367.6; on the AT between Indian Gap and Newfound Gap in GSMNP; and along the C&O Canal in Maryland.

WOOD ANEMONE

Anemone quinquefolia

As an early spring flower, Wood Anemone has developed a mechanism to compensate for the small number of pollinating insects alive at that time of year. By producing an over-abundance of pollen it assures that, if no insects visit, wind will carry at least some of the pollen to nearby plants and fertilize them. This is one reason why you may find large patches of the plants growing along forest borders, one of their favored environments. Once pollination occurs, a hairy, seedlike fruit develops and, soon afterward, the leaves die back and aboveground signs of the plant disappear.

A fanciful story from Greece tells of the Anemone's origin. Zephyr, god of the west wind, became enamored of a nymph named Anemone. Jealous of their love, Flora, goddess of flowers, turned Anemone into a flower that was ever after fated to bloom early and fade quickly.

The species name *quinquefolia* ("leaves of five") refers to the basal leaves, which are divided into three to five leaflets.

Other common names for Wood Anemone, which is one of the most abundant of Anemones in the area, include Windflower, Nimbleweed, Woodflower, and Wild Cucumber. Mountain Anemone (*Anemone lancifolia*) has similar blossoms but grows up to sixteen inches high and has only a whorl of leaves a short distance below the flower and no basal leaflets. Less common, and blooming from June to August, Tall Anemone (*Anemone virginiana*), also known as Thimbleweed because of the thimble shape of its fruit, may reach two to three feet in height.

Some places you may encounter Wood Anemone or Mountain Anemone include: Bradley Fork and Abrams Forks Trails, and Laurel Creek Road in GSMNP; Skyline Nature Trail in Chimney Rock Park in Chimney Rock, North Carolina; BRP mileposts 176.2, 179.3, 230.1, 427.5, and 453.4; and in the higher elevations of Catoctin Mountain Park in Maryland.

FOAMFLOWER

Tiarella cordifolia

FLOWER:
   The quarter-inch white flowers grow in clusters at the end of a (usually) leafless, six- to twelve-inch raceme. Each flower has five tapering petals and ten very long, very conspicuous stamens tipped with orange or red anthers.

LEAVES AND STEM:
   Growing on long stalks, the two- to four-inch basal leaves are round- to heart-shaped. Sharply toothed edges and three to seven shallow lobes make the leaves resemble maple leaves. The upper surfaces are hairy, while the undersides may be smooth or slightly downy. The plant rises on a stem than can grow close to one foot.

BLOOM SEASON:
   April to June

Foamflower is a member of the Saxifrage family, a diverse group of close to 700 species primarily found in the temperate and cooler regions of the Northern Hemisphere. Gray's *Manual of Botany* lists more than sixty species in the eastern part of North America. Among them are Hydrangeas, Gooseberries, Currants, Alumroots, Ditch Stonecrop, Grass-of-Parnassus (*Parnassia asarifolia;* see page 92), Carolina Saxifrage, Early Saxifrage, Michaux's Saxifrage (*Saxifraga michauxii;* see page 72), and False Goatsbeard.

When seen from a distance, Foamflower can resemble the froth on a good head of beer bubbling up from the rich woodlands, the disturbed soil of pathways and roads, and the environment along mountain stream banks that it tends to favor. This explains its common name, while the species name *cordifolia* refers to the heart-shaped base of the leaves that turn bronze in the fall.

Because its leaves resemble those of the Miterwort, Foamflower is sometimes referred to as False Miterwort. However, the flowers are distinctly different. Both are white and small, not much more than a quarter inch in size, but the five tapering petals of Foamflower look quite different from the Miterwort's fringed petals. In addition, Foamflower's ten pistils are long and conspicuous, while Miterwort's pistils are hidden inside the flower's small cup, or bladder.

Some places you may encounter Foamflower include: around Deep Creek Campground, Little River Road, and along Sugarlands Nature, Bradley Fork, and Cosby Nature Trails in GSMNP; BRP mileposts 296.9, 339.5, and 367.7; and on the AT south of the Nantahala River, north of Winding Stair Gap, and between High Rocks and Spivey Gap in North Carolina.

WILD STONECROP

Sedum ternatum

FLOWER:
Arranged in a floral spray along (usually) three (often curving) horizontal branches, the half-inch-wide, star-shaped flowers have five white, narrow-pointed petals, ten stamens with dark anthers, and several green sepals.

LEAVES AND STEM:
The round- to spoon-shaped leaves are smooth and thick, and grow in whorls of three on the portion of the stem that creeps along the ground. The leaves on the upper part of the stem, which rises toward the floral sprays, grow singly. A number of leaf bracts appear just below the petals of the flowers.

BLOOM SEASON:
April to June

Most references state that Wild Stonecrop received its genus name, *Sedum,* from the way it spreads across the ground and comes "to sit" on boulders, rocks, and logs. In *Garden Flower Folklore,* Laura C. Martin tells another story of the name's origin. She says the name came from the Romans who grew the plant on their rooftops in the belief that it would ward off lightning, and that the name is derived from the Latin word *seob,* meaning "allay" or "calm."

Wild Stonecrop is such an interesting plant that it warrants getting down on hands and knees to inspect closely. The dark, almost black, anthers sitting atop the flower's ten stamens contrast with the white petals (accounting for another common name, Pepper and Salt). But look closer and you will find that the plant has both fertile and sterile stems. Those that are fertile have a whorl of basal leaves and additional leaves that alternate along the stems. The sterile stems' succulent leaves occur in whorls of three, giving rise to the species name *ternatum,* meaning "coming together in threes."

Several other Stonecrops grow in the Blue Ridge and Great Smoky Mountains. American Orpine or Allegheny Stonecrop (*Sedum telephioides*) has pink flowers and oblong leaves. With purplish-pink flowers, Wild Live Forever (*Sedum purpureum*), a name sometimes also used for American Orpine, is an import from Europe and received its common name from its ability to produce a new plant from almost any part of the parent plant.

Some places you may encounter one of the Stonecrops include: The Pocket on Pigeon Mountain in Walker County, Georgia; Little River Road and Chestnut Top and Huskey Gap Trails in GSMNP; BRP milepost 63.6; on the AT on the north slope of Pearis Mountain in southwest Virginia and Tinker Cliffs and Humpback Mountain in central Virginia; and Hawksbill and along Rose River Fire Road in SNP.

CATESBY'S TRILLIUM

Trillium catesbaei

The two- to three-inch-wide flower (usually) nods below the leaves. The three white (sometimes pink) petals are curved sharply backward, while the three narrow sepals have been described as sickle-shaped. The stamens, which have long filaments, are tipped with golden anthers.

The one- to three-inch leaves are broadly oval-shaped, taper sharply at the tips, and are finely veined. They are stalked and grow on a stem that is eight to twenty inches tall.

April to June

Several varieties of Trilliums are common throughout the Blue Ridge and Great Smoky Mountains, but consider yourself lucky if you come upon a patch of Catesby's Trillium. It grows, in not very large numbers, only in the southern portion of the region. The species name honors Mark Catesby, an English naturalist who explored the southern Appalachian Mountains and southeastern North America around the turn of the seventeenth century.

Because its petals turn to pink as the flower ages (or sometimes are pink from the very beginning), Catesby's Trillium is sometimes mistaken for Large-Flowered Trillium (*Trillium grandiflorum;* see page 252), whose blossoms may go through the same change in color.

Of the other Trilliums found in the region, Purple Trillium (*Trillium erectum;* see page 252) is probably the most common. Sweet White Trillium (*Trillium simile;* see page 252) has broad, ovate, white petals with a dark ovary in the center; it sometimes has dark pink to red petals. The white petals of Painted Trillium (*Trillium undulatum;* see page 253) have splashes of purple and crinkly edges. Like Catesby's Trillium, Vasey's Trillium (*Trillium vaseyi;* see page 253), which has a (usually) nodding purple blossom, is found in the Blue Ridge and Great Smoky Mountains only in Georgia, North Carolina, and Tennessee.

Some of the places you may encounter one of the Trilliums include: Pinhoti Trail in Floyd County, Georgia; Rich Mountain, Tremont, Greenbrier, Balsam Mountain, and Newfound Gap Roads, and Cades Cove Nature, Lower Mount Cammerer, and Cove Hardwood Nature Trails, and Chimneys Picnic Area in GSMNP; BRP mileposts 175, 176.2, 200–216, 294, 298.9, 333, and 364.6; and on the AT between Max Patch and Hot Springs in North Carolina, north of Angel's Rest in southwest Virginia, Petites Gap, Thunder Ridge, and The Priest in central Virginia.

MAYAPPLE

Podophyllum peltatum

FLOWER:
A single, waxy, nodding, white flower grows from the middle of the fork of the two leaves. About an inch wide, the flower has more than a dozen stamens with yellow anthers that emerge from the center of six to nine petals.

LEAVES AND STEM:
Rising to about a foot, the two umbrella-like, toothed leaves are divided into five to seven lobes. Plants with only one leaf do not bear flowers.

BLOOM SEASON:
April to June

Mayapple is also known as Mandrake because European emigrants who had settled in North America's eastern mountains found that the plant's roots were reminiscent of those of *Mandragora officinarium,* a member of the Nightshade family that grows in both Europe and Asia. Many of these settlers believed in the Doctrine of Signatures, which states that a plant cures whatever ails the body part that it resembles. Since Mayapple's roots are shaped somewhat like the human body, as are those of Ginseng (*Panax quinquefolius*), it was considered an overall health remedy.

Modern medicine obtains podophyllin from Mayapple to be used as a purgative and in the treatment of venereal disorders and cancer.

With leaves looking like miniature beach umbrellas stuck haphazardly in the soil, scores of Mayapple plants can form carpets that spread across large expanses of the forest floor. Like the leaves of the Bloodroot (*Sanguinaria canadensis;* see page 14), the leaves of the Mayapple are tightly wound around the stem as the plant pushes its way through the soil.

Some people find the flower's smell quite repugnant, while others say that after it has been on the plant for a while it has a pleasing fragrance. The apple, which can develop from the flower as early as June, looks more like a green, oval-shaped berry than an apple.

Some places you may encounter Mayapple include: Little River and Cove Hardwood Nature and Porters Creek Trails in GSMNP; BRP mileposts 76.4, 163, 176.2, 339.5, and 435.2; on the AT between Neels Gap and Unicoi Gap in Georgia, and on Thunder Ridge in central Virginia; along Jack-O-Lantern Branch Trail in Booker T. Washington National Monument, Virginia; and in the higher elevations of Catoctin Mountain Park in Maryland.

UMBRELLA LEAF

Diphylleia cymosa

Growing in terminal clusters above the leaves, the white flowers are about three-quarters of an inch wide, have six oval-shaped petals, six stamens, and one pistil. The six sepals may be absent, as they fall off soon after the blossom develops.

Non-flowering plants have a single, umbrella-like leaf that can be up to two feet wide. It is attached to the two- to four-foot stem in the middle of the leaf. The two leaves of flowering plants are just a bit smaller, coarsely toothed, and deeply cleft in the middle.

April to June

Umbrella Leaf is a member of the Barberry family, which Roger Tory Peterson says is a grouping of dissimilar plants that are lumped together for technical reasons. Worldwide, there are about a dozen genera and 650 species, but fewer than ten species are found in the eastern United States. Among them are Mayapple (*Podophyllum peltatum;* see page 32), Blue Cohosh, and Twinleaf.

Like Catesby's Trillium (*Trillium catesbaei;* see page 30), Umbrella Leaf is a plant that is confined to the southern portion of the Blue Ridge and Great Smoky Mountains, growing no farther north than western Virginia. Also like the Catesby's Trillium, it is not very common, and you should consider yourself lucky to come across it. Look for it in the deep shade of cool forest coves beside mountain springs and streams or close to the seeps on wet, rocky slopes.

Although encountered infrequently in the Blue Ridge and Great Smoky Mountain area, an almost identical species is found so abundantly in China and throughout the alps of Japan that it is harvested and used as a treatment for cancer.

Many observers feel that Umbrella Leaf is at its most charming after the flowers have faded away and developed into round or oval berries whose deep blue stands out against the bright scarlet of their stalks and the changing color of the leaves.

Some places you may encounter Umbrella Leaf include: Balsam Mountain and Newfound Gap Roads, Little River Trail, and on US 441 between Newfound Gap and Gatlinburg in GSMNP; and on the pathway close to the Linn Cove Observation Platform and Information Center at BRP milepost 304.4.

GARLIC MUSTARD

Alliaria petiolata

FLOWER:
Several of the quarter-inch, four-petaled, cross-shaped flowers are clustered at the tips of the stems.

LEAVES AND STEM:
The one- to six-inch leaves are sharply toothed, triangular- to heart-shaped, and attached with long stalks alternately along the one- to three-foot stem.

BLOOM SEASON:
April to June

Garlic Mustard, with its small white flower clusters, has become such a common plant of the Appalachian Mountains since it was brought from Europe that you may walk by it without even noticing it. It has spread so quickly that it now covers large portions of the forest floor and is considered an invasive plant in some areas because it is crowding out many of the native wildflowers, such as Bloodroot (*Sanguinaria canadensis;* see page 14) and Dutchman's-Breeches (*Dicentra cucullaria;* see page 18).

There are more than thirty different insects in Europe that feed upon the leaves, stems, and seeds of the Garlic Mustard. This plant, like most exotic species that are introduced into an area, has spread and become a problem in North America because there are no natural predators here. The plants also produce a prodigious amount of seeds.

Other common names, including Hedge Garlic, Sauce-All-Alone, Garlic Root, and Poor Man's Mustard, provide insight as to why the plant was originally imported. The garlic–onion flavored leaves have been eaten for centuries in salads and sauces and used as potherbs or seasonings for meat dishes. A simple recipe that uses the plant as a substitute for greens says to boil both the leaves and flowers for ten minutes, drain the water, and boil and drain again before adding butter, pepper, and nutmeg.

The leaves have also been used medicinally. Believing they possessed antiseptic properties, herbalists crushed and applied them directly to wounds and open sores. In 1755 Sir John Hill, in *The Family Herbal,* said to boil them and mix the water with honey to treat sore throats and coughs.

Some places you may encounter Garlic Mustard include: BRP mileposts 8.8, 17.6, 22.2, 44.4, 63.6, 74.9, 110.9, 133.6, 168, 176.2, and 179.3.

WILD STRAWBERRY
Fragaria virginiana

FLOWER:
  The three-quarter-inch white flowers have five rounded petals, five sepals, and many pistils and stamens tipped with yellow anthers.

LEAVES AND STEM:
  The one- to one-and-a-half-inch leaves are coarsely toothed and divided into three leaflets that are attached to hairy stems that may be as much as six inches tall.

BLOOM SEASON:
  April to June

Oh, the joy of finding a patch of Wild Strawberries! The juicy concentration of flavor within these tiny little marvels puts their cultivated relatives, which are a cross between this species and one found in South America, to shame. Contrary to popular belief, the red, watery bulb of flesh, the "berry," is not the fruit of the plant, but rather the enlarged end of the stem to which the flower was attached, known in botanical terms as the "receptacle." Those little things that look like seeds and are embedded in pits on the outer surface of the "berry" are the actual fruits and are referred to as "achenes" by botanists.

Wild Strawberry propagates itself not only by seeds but also by sending out horizontal stems that take root at their tips. From these, new leaves form and another plant begins to grow. The dried leaves can be made into a savory tea that is full of vitamin C.

Several stories tell how the plant earned its common name. One says the name comes from the Anglo-Saxon word *streow*, meaning "stray," which strawberries certainly do via their runners. Another claims hay or straw was once placed under the plants to keep the berries from getting dirty in the soil, while some sources say that the name comes from medieval times when the fruits were strung on straws and hung in the marketplace.

Some places you may encounter Wild Strawberry include: Parson Bald, Bradley Fork Trail, Rich Mountain Road, and Fightin' Creek Gap in GSMNP; Hooper Bald and Huckleberry Knob along the Cherohala Skyway in North Carolina; BRP mileposts 8.8, 17.6, 55.1, 74.9, 139, 162.4, 202.8, 242.3, 326, 380, 411, 435.2, and 457.9; on the AT on Cold Mountain in central Virginia; Jackson River Gorge Trail in Bath County, Virginia; and along the roads of Catoctin Mountain Park in Maryland.

FAIRY WAND

Chameaelirium luteum

FLOWER:
Growing in a dense raceme, the tiny white flowers have three petals and three sepals.

LEAVES AND STEM:
The ovate evergreen basal leaves are three to eight inches long. Those that grow along the one- to four-foot stem are much smaller and slenderer.

BLOOM SEASON:
April to July

If any one plant ever had a batch of inconsistent common names, it would have to be *Chameaelirium luteum*. Based upon the way the long raceme of white flowers looks, the name Fairy Wand brings to mind pleasant images of a benevolent sprite granting wish after wish for us. With the long racemes of the male flowers curling around like a part of a horse's harness, Devil's Bit conjures up horrible scenes of Beelzebub riding after us on a charging steed, hoping to catch us and wrench our souls into Hades, while Blazing Star may bring about heavenly thoughts. Unicorn Root returns us to fanciful mythological creatures, but Rattlesnake Root blocks out any urge to meet up with its slithering namesake.

Even the genus name is inconsistent. Although *lirium* is from the Greek *lierion* and identifies the plant as being a Lily, the other part of the name comes from the word *chamai*, which translates as "lay on the ground," something the flowers certainly do not do.

Male and female flowers grow on separate plants. The female flowers, with their pistils, are greenish-white and grow on a raceme that remains erect. The male flowers are white and fluffy-looking because of the numerous yellow stamens. They grow on racemes that are shorter and have a tendency to curl or bend over.

The plants are a favorite of gardeners; in the wild they are found in both bright sun and partial shade but will only grow if the soil is rich and moist.

Some places you may encounter Fairy Wand include: Cades Cove Road in GSMNP; and Dragon's Tooth Trail in Craig County, Virginia.

BLADDER CAMPION

Silene cucubalus

FLOWER:

The five white petals that grow on the opening of the inflated calyx (the bladder) are so deeply cleft that there can almost appear to be ten petals. The ten stamens grow from deep inside the calyx and are tipped with brown anthers.

LEAVES AND STEM:

The one- to four-inch oblong to lanceolate leaves sometimes clasp the stem on which they grow oppositely. The stem can reach a height of almost two feet.

BLOOM SEASON:

April to August

There is disagreement among authorities as to the origin of Bladder Campion's name. Some say that the word "campion" comes from the Latin *campus,* meaning "field," where Bladder Campion often grows. Others point out that it may derive from *campione,* or "battlefield," to reflect the fact that some species of the plant were used in garlands or chaplets given to the victors, or "champions," of public games or tournaments that simulated the skills needed in warfare.

The plant's interesting, thin-textured, almost translucent bladder, which has been compared to a melon or a fat tear, has also given rise to a number of other common and fanciful names, including Rattle-Bags, Fairy Potatoes, and Bird's Eggs. Bladder Campion's inflated calyx is smooth, which helps differentiate it from the hairy bladder of White Campion (*Silene latifolia;* see page 253), whose five petals are fatter and not as deeply cleft. The five petals of Starry Campion (*Silene stellata*) are so deeply fringed that they appear to be many separate petals.

Because members of this genus have sticky hairs that often capture insects, the plants are also called Catchfly. Within the Blue Ridge and Great Smoky Mountains you may encounter Forking Catchfly (*Silene dichotoma*), which has a stalkless calyx and much slenderer leaves. Night-Flowering Catchfly (*Silene noctiflora*) has broader leaves. Fire Pink (*Silene virginica;* see page 166) is considered by many to be the most colorful of the genus.

When looking to other sources for information on Bladder Campion, you should be aware that some reference books list it as *Silene vulgaris.*

Some places you may encounter a plant within the *Silene* genus include: Noland Divide and Chestnut Top Trails in GSMNP; Chunky Gal Trail in Clay County, North Carolina; BRP mileposts 8.8, 17.6, 78.4, 132.9, 176.2, and 376–381; and along the Chessie Nature Trail near Lexington, Virginia.

SMOOTH
SOLOMON'S SEAL

Polygonatum biflorum

FLOWER:
The half-inch, greenish-white, bell-shaped flowers of the Smooth Solomon's Seal droop from the leaf axils, usually in pairs.

LEAVES AND STEM:
The sessile (meaning they have no stalk) leaves are arranged alternately on the one- to three-foot arching stem.

BLOOM SEASON:
May to June

Some reference books place the Solomon's Seals within the green flower category, some within the yellow, and others among the plants that have white flowers. Truth be told, the Solomon's Seals belong in all three groupings. As the flowers emerge they definitely have a greenish tinge to them, which becomes a greenish-yellow as they develop. At maturity, the color will have faded to a greenish-white.

The genus name *Polygonatum* comes from the Greek language and means "many knees," a reference to the joints and bends in the plant's underground roots.

Of the several species found in the Blue Ridge and Great Smoky Mountains, possibly the most common is the Smooth Solomon's Seal. A subspecies, Great Solomon's Seal (*Polygonatum biflorum commutatum,* which some sources list as *Polygonatum biflorum canaliculatum*) is the largest, with the longest leaves, longest stem, and most numerous flowers dangling from the leaf axils. The Hairy Solomon's Seal (*Polygonatum pubescens*) can be distinguished by the hairs that grow on the underside of the leaves along the veins. Looking somewhat like the Solomon's Seals, Rosy Twisted Stalk (*Streptopus roseus;* see page 162) has a bent or crooked stem and pink-tinted flowers. The leaves of False Solomon's Seal (*Smilacina racemosa;* see page 50) have a similar appearance, but its flowers grow at the end of the stem.

Some places you may encounter one of the Solomon's Seals include: Sosebee Cove in Union County, Georgia; Yellow Mountain Trail in Jackson County, North Carolina; Little River Gorge, and Roaring Fork Motor Nature and Porters Creek Trails in GSMNP; BRP milepost 272; on the AT on Blood Mountain in Georgia, between High Rocks and Spivey Gap in North Carolina, and north of John's Spring Shelter and in Petites Gap in central Virginia; and Lostland Run Trail in Garrett County, Maryland.

STARFLOWER

Trientalis borealis

The two frail white flowers of the Starflower have six to seven pointed petals and seven golden anther–tipped stamens. Each flower is at the top of a thin and easily broken stalk.

A whorl of seven to nine leaves grows below the pair of flowers. The lance-shaped leaves, pointed on both sides, can vary quite widely in size, growing anywhere from one and a half inches to more than four inches.

May to June

Whereas Catesby's Trillium (*Trillium catesbaei;* see page 30) and Umbrella Leaf (*Diphylleia cymosa;* see page 34) are confined to the southern portion of the Blue Ridge and Great Smoky Mountains, most botanists identify Starflower as an infrequent inhabitant of the more northern sections. However—as in the rest of nature where there are few, if any, hard and fast rules—these lovely flowers have been seen in southern Virginia, North Carolina, and Tennessee, and there have even been reports of it growing as far south as the summit of Blood Mountain in north Georgia.

The species name *borealis* reflects its preference for the cooler temperatures of higher elevations or more northern climates, such as Nova Scotia, Newfoundland, and Labrador, where it thrives. Like so many other plants that have adapted themselves to harsh conditions, Starflower is a creeping plant (which explains why you usually see patches of it) that sends up erect branches that are rarely more than eight to nine inches tall. This low height helps prevent damage from high winds and ice storms, while the shallow-growing rootstocks make it one of the first plants to take advantage of any moisture that seeps into the ground.

In addition to propagating itself through the division of its roots, Starflower, also commonly called Chickweed Wintergreen, produces seeds that develop inside the fruit and force their way out by splitting the capsule along its seams.

Some places you may encounter Starflower include: on the AT on Blood Mountain in Georgia, and between Floyd Mountain and Parkers Gap in central Virginia.

SPECKLED WOOD LILY

Clintonia umbellulata

FLOWER:
The half-inch flowers, which grow in an umbel at the top of a thin, eight- to twenty-inch stalk, have three white petals and three white petal-like sepals that are usually dotted with green and purple.

LEAVES AND STEM:
The oval-shaped, hairy leaves grow in a basal whorl.

BLOOM SEASON:
May to July

Clintonia umbellulata has a number of common names, and all of them are justly deserved and describe some aspect of the plant. An inhabitant of rich moist forests, this member of the Lily family has white flower petals marked by small purple and green spots, so what could be more descriptive than Speckled Wood Lily? Sometime in midsummer the petals of the flowers fall off and are replaced by small clusters of shiny dark blue (almost black) berries that resemble beads and give rise to another common name, Bead Lily. This may lead to its being confused with a similarly named relative, Bluebead Lily (*Clintonia borealis;* see page 120). Although they can look inviting, the berries of neither plant should be eaten, as they are poisonous.

The genus name *Clintonia* and two other common names, White Clintonia and Clinton's Lily, honor De Witt Clinton, a governor of New York, a proponent of the Erie Canal, and a dedicated naturalist who wrote a number of noted books on natural history and science. *Clintonia* first appeared in Asa Gray's *Manual of Botany.* However, Gray states that he did not come up with the name and gives credit to Samuel Constantine Rafinesque, a professor at Transylvania University in Lexington, Kentucky.

The species name *umbellulata* is also descriptive in that the flowers grow in an umbel atop a long stalk.

Some places you may encounter Speckled Wood Lily include: Black Mountain Crest Trail in Yancey County, North Carolina; Roaring Fork Motor Nature and Noland Divide Trails, and near Rainbow Falls in GSMNP; BRP mileposts 167.1, 169, 217.9, and 431; on the AT near Laurel Falls in Tennessee, Thunder Hill in central Virginia, and Compton Gap in SNP; and Shamokin Nature Preserve in Wintergreen Resort, Virginia.

FALSE SOLOMON'S SEAL

Smilacina racemosa

In recent years there has been a call by some wildflower enthusiasts to stop using the word "false" in the names of plants. After all, is not a plant a plant in its own right? For this reason you may increasingly come across some resources that list False Solomon's Seal as Solomon's Plume or, to a lesser extent, Solomon's Zigzag or Job's Tears.

This dissatisfaction with the word "false" is not new; there were people as early as the 1800s urging that it not be used. In the 1895 publication of *Familiar Flowers of Field and Garden,* F. Schuyler Matthews proclaimed of the False Solomon's Seal: "Why should not a plant so deserving have its own good name? We might as well call a Frenchman a false Englishman! It seems as though our nation was lacking in both originality and imagination!"

The species name *racemosa* refers to the way the flowers grow in a terminal cluster, or raceme. *Smilacina* is Greek for "rough" and alludes to the hairs along the plant's stem.

A species that is found in this range only in the Virginia mountains, Star-Flowered False Solomon's Seal (*Smilacina stellata*) has a shorter stem than the False Solomon's Seal, its star-shaped flowers are larger, and its leaves clasp the stem.

When looking to other sources for information about the False Solomon's Seals, you should be aware that some books place them within the genus *Maianthemum,* Greek for "May flower."

Some places you may encounter False Solomon's Seal include: Sosebee Cove in Union County, Georgia; Little River Gorge, Cove Hardwood Nature Trail, and Tremont Road in GSMNP; BRP mileposts 63.6, 168, 218.7, 260.3, 308.2, and 359.9; on the AT on Little Bald along the North Carolina–Tennessee border, north of John's Spring Shelter, in Petites Gap, and along Humpback Mountain in central Virginia; Crabtree Falls Trail in Nelson County, Virginia; and the upland woods in Catoctin Mountain Park in Maryland.

COMMON WOOD SORREL

Oxalis montana

FLOWER:

Somewhat resembling those of the Spring Beauty (Claytonia virginica; see page 152), the flowers of the Wood Sorrel have five white—sometimes pale pink—petals that are marked with very noticeable dark pink to purple veins and are (usually) notched at the tips.

LEAVES AND STEM:

The basal leaves are divided into three heart-shaped segments that join together to form a shamrock or clover shape.

BLOOM SEASON:

May to July

There is something magical about walking into the rich, shaded retreat of a southern Appalachian woodlands. The air is moist, the forest floor is soft and damp, mosses tint the scene with luminous hues of green, and lush vegetation of all sizes keeps your eyes moving from one marvelous shape to another. If you are lucky, the shamrock-shaped leaves of the Wood Sorrel will have added to the enchantment of the place by creating a carpet that covers nearly every inch of ground—lumps and folds marking where the plants have grown upon rocks, boulders, and fallen trees.

Be sure to linger here and investigate your surroundings a bit more; the natural world will reward you with a delectation that eludes the casual visitor. Look beyond the Wood Sorrel's pink-veined petals and you will find the plant's hidden secret. Located below the leaves and close to the base of the plant is a cleistogamous flower, a blossom that never opens up but self-pollinates and produces another set of seeds to help insure propagation of the species.

Wood Sorrel is also known as Sour Grass, a reference to the oxalic acid (hence, its genus name *Oxalis*) that imparts a somewhat tart, lemony taste to its leaves.

When looking to other sources for information about the Common Wood Sorrel, you should be aware that it has undergone a change in its name and that some reference books refer to it as *Oxalis acetosella*.

Some places you may encounter Common Wood Sorrel include: Clingmans Dome Road, and Spruce-Fir Nature and Forney Ridge Trails in GSMNP; Joyce Kilmer Memorial Trail in Joyce Kilmer–Slickrock Wilderness in North Carolina; Mount Rogers Spur Trail in Smyth and Grayson Counties, and Slabcamp Run Trail in Highland County, Virginia; on the AT on Fork Mountain in central Virginia; and Swallow Falls State Park in Maryland.

GALAX
Galax aphylla

The extremely small white flowers are clustered on a naked, one- to two-foot-high stalk.

The heart-shaped (almost round), toothed, shiny green leaves grow close to the ground.

May to July

Use your imagination a little bit and Galax's tiny white flowers clustered around the top of its stalk can appear to be small stars bursting from the wand that a fairy has just waved while chanting an incantation to carpet the forest floor with lush green, heart-shaped leaves.

Galax was once a ubiquitous plant in the Blue Ridge and Great Smoky Mountains, but its foliage became its own worst enemy as humans found it useful: around the turn of the twentieth century, mountain people supplemented their meager incomes by picking the plants and selling them to commercial florists who favored them for arrangements because the leaves stay green long after being pulled from the soil.

The practice faded away for a few decades but returned with a vengeance in the late 1900s. No longer picked casually by local families, bands of organized poachers scour the mountains and harvest Galax in such large numbers that the plant is now in danger. On one occasion, rangers on the Blue Ridge Parkway arrested three people who, in the course of a single day, had picked more than 70,000 stems of Galax. The problem has become so pervasive that authorities are using a powdered marker developed for the explosives industry to mark plants so that they can be identified when trying to be sold. Hidden electronics and cameras are employed to alert law enforcement officials who hope to catch the culprits before they get away. Because of this problem, it was decided not to include in this book specific sites where you may encounter Galax in the Blue Ridge and Great Smoky Mountains.

When looking to other sources for information about Galax, you should be aware that some books list it as *Galax urceolata*. In addition, the fact that other references refer to the plant as *Galax rotundifolia* indicate that it has undergone an additional name change.

GOATSBEARD

Aruncus dioicus

Because of its height, showy flower spikes, and large leaves—and the fact that it is a very common plant of the forest that grows well in wet ravines, seeps, and borders—Goatsbeard is a plant not easy to overlook and one that is valued by horticulturists for its robust appearance. The spikes of flowers, which some people say resemble the flowing whiskers under a billy goat's chin, arch over like feathery plumes, giving the plant one of its other common names, Bride's Feathers. In the fall, the leaves turn a brilliant yellow, providing a colorful background for later-blooming plants.

But it takes a magnifying glass to truly appreciate the beauty and interesting nature of its blossoms, which average less than an eighth inch in width. The species name *dioicus* means that the plant is dioecious, that is, that male and female flowers grow on separate plants. The male bloom has fifteen or more white stamens, while the female has three or four pistils and numerous tiny, undeveloped stamens. Some people theorize that this indicates that at some time in the past Goatsbeard had both female and male parts on the same plant.

Cherokee Indians pounded the root into a poultice to treat bee stings. A tea made from the root was used to soak and relieve the pain of swollen feet; it was also drunk to reduce polyuria or diminish bleeding after childbirth.

False Goatsbeard (*Astilbe biternata*) is similar in appearance, but it has a lobed terminal leaf and flowers with only ten stamens.

Some places you may encounter Goatsbeard include: Heintooga Ridge and Rich Mountain Roads, and Noland Divide Trail in GSMNP; Cherohala Skyway in North Carolina; BRP mileposts 10–11, 24, 240, 337.6, and 370–375; and Skyline Drive milepost 64.5 in SNP.

NEW JERSEY TEA

Ceanothus americanus

FLOWER:

Borne in dense, cylindrical clusters that are about a half inch in diameter and one inch long, the individual flowers are no more than one-fifth of an inch wide. Each blossom has five greenish-white petals, five tiny erect stamens, and a pistil with a three-lobed style that rises from the middle of the flower.

LEAVES AND STEM:

The two- to four-inch leaves occur alternately on the stem and are ovate, pointed, toothed, curved around the edges, hairy above, and paler and downy underneath.

BLOOM SEASON:

May to July or August

New Jersey Tea is a shrub that grows to one to three feet (and in rare instances, to four feet). The stem is woody with greenish-brown bark that flakes off as it ages. The clusters of white flowers rise on long stalks from the leaf axils of new growth, which appear to be herbaceous rather than woody.

It is believed that Native Americans taught the early colonists how to use the leaves to make a tea that became popular as a substitute for black tea during the Revolutionary War—drinking it was a gesture of patriotism in the fledgling country. Because the plant was common and the leaves readily available for harvest, American soldiers were some of the most frequent drinkers of the brew as they marched from place to place.

Native Americans also made a red tea from the roots (hence, another common name, Red Root) to treat colds, stomach ailments, and diarrhea. They must have known what they were doing, as modern science has found the roots to contain as much as ten percent tannins, effective astringent substances. Some herbalists today still suggest using Red Root as a cough medicine and to soothe sore throats.

Humans are not the only ones to find New Jersey Tea useful. The leaves are a favorite food of white-tailed deer, and wild turkeys browse on the three-lobed, three-seeded fruits whose distinctive cup-shaped bases stay on the plant well into winter.

Some places you may encounter New Jersey Tea include: Cades Cove in GSMNP; and BRP mileposts 38.8, 42–43, 91–100, 138.4, 197, 211, 235, 241, and 328.6.

YARROW

Achillea millefolium

FLOWER:
The white (sometimes pink) flowers have four to six rays that occur in numerous dense terminal clusters.

LEAVES AND STEM:
The finely divided leaves can be as much as ten inches long and grow on single or divided stems of one to three feet in height.

BLOOM SEASON:
May to October

Along with Black-Eyed Susan (*Rudbeckia hirta;* see page 132), Chicory (*Cicorium intybus;* see page 234), and other members of the Aster (also known as Composite or Daisy) family, Yarrow may be seen along roads and in overgrown meadows throughout much of the growing season. The blossoms may be what attract you from a distance, but your eyes will probably be drawn to the leaves once you get closer to the plant. Growing alternately on the stem, they are so finely divided that they resemble fern fronds, and the species name *millefolium,* which means "thousand leaves," reflects their appearance. In botanical terms, they are known as "bipinnate" leaves, meaning that they branch off the main stem and then branch again into smaller leaflets.

For more than a millennium, Yarrow was used as an astringent to stop the flow of blood, and the genus name *Achillea* honors the Greek hero Achilles who, according to legend, used the plant to treat battle-wounded comrades. This story may be the stuff of legend, but what is certainly true is that physicians on both sides of the Civil War gathered Yarrow as armies marched by fields and meadows, and used it to successfully save many an injured soldier.

Some scholars claim that Yarrow is native to the North American plains, while others argue that it is an import from Europe. Regardless of its origins, if you see one Yarrow plant today you are most likely going to see scores of them. It occurs in such great numbers because it reproduces not only by being fertilized by insects that transfer pollen from plant to plant, but by spreading across the land via underground runners.

Some places you may encounter Yarrow include: Cades Cove and other meadows in GSMNP; BRP mileposts 17.6, 81.9, 110.9, 154.5, 189.1, 232.5, 281.5, 326.0, 373.9, 427.5, and 467.8; on the AT on Max Patch in North Carolina; and along roads in Catoctin Mountain Park in Maryland.

QUEEN ANNE'S LACE

Daucus carota

Queen Anne's Lace is an import from Europe now found in every state of the continental United States. A close look at its cluster of flowers, known as an umbel, will reveal how it has been able to spread so far and wide.

The umbel, growing from the main stem, is made up of smaller umbels, or umbellets, rising on individual stalks that emanate from the same point on the main stem. Each stalk divides again, and the individual flowers grow on these smaller stalks. Each floret has five petals, five stamens, and a pistil growing in the center. The outside blossoms of the outside umbellets have petals larger than the inner blossoms.

When the flowers wither and the fruits begin to form, each umbellet curves toward the center, and threadlike bracts pull the entire umbel into a tight, brown cluster, earning the plant one of its other common names, Bird's Nest. Studies have shown that these mature umbels can contain more than 800 seeds—and each plant may have as many as a dozen such "bird's nests."

This plethora of seeds is not the only mechanism that Queen Anne's Lace has developed to insure survival. Birds do not like the spiny seeds, and insects and browsing animals avoid eating the rough and acrid-tasting foliage and stem. Also, freezing temperatures cannot reach the plant's long taproot, growing deep in the soil, where it stores up the starchy food that it will use to burst forth early next season.

Some places you may encounter Queen Anne's Lace include: roads in Floyd County, Georgia; Cades Cove in GSMNP; BRP mileposts 17.6, 78.4, 154.1, 189.1, 259, 277.9, 399.7, and 467.8; Fairwood Valley Trail in Smyth County and Rhododendron Trail in Grayson Highlands State Park in Virginia; on the AT on Max Patch in North Carolina, and Peters Mountain in central Virginia; roads in Catoctin Mountain Park, and Snaggy Mountain Road in Garrett State Forest in Maryland.

GREAT
RHODODENDRON

Rhododendron maximum

FLOWERS:
 The white to light pink flowers are about two inches across, are open bell–shaped, have five lobes, and grow in large and ornate clusters.

LEAVES AND STEM:
 The four- to eight-inch-long distinctive oblong, shiny, leathery, evergreen leaves grow on shrubs that usually range from five to fifteen feet in height.

BLOOM SEASON:
 June to July

When the Great Rhododendron (also called Rosebay Rhododendron) shrubs begin to bloom in mid-June, the flowers first appear as tightly closed, rich pink pods but soon open into large, white blossoms. Take a close look and you will notice that the uppermost petal of each bloom is decorated by small, green dots. It is believed that this colorful pattern helps guide insects to the pollen.

Also found within the Blue Ridge and Great Smoky Mountains is Carolina Rhododendron (*Rhododendron minus*), whose leaves are smaller and dotted brown underneath. Catawba Rhododendron (*Rhododendron catawbiensis*; see page 253) has flowers whose colors range from light pink to dark pink to rich purple; they bloom about a month before those of the Great Rhododendron.

If you are outdoors in winter, you can use the plants' leaves to determine the temperature. In order to protect their soft undersides from the desiccating effects of cool breezes, the leaves begin to droop and curl under. The tighter the curl, the colder it is. When the leaves are wrapped around themselves to about the size of a choice cigar, the temperature is hovering around freezing; the diameter of a cheap cigar means that it is getting into the twenties and the teens. If you see that the leaves have become no larger than a cigarette, you had better be wearing lots of layers—the temperature is mighty close to zero.

Some places you may encounter one of the Rhododendrons include: Joyce Kilmer Memorial Forest, and NC 209 south of Hot Springs in North Carolina; Mount Rogers Trail in Smyth County and Lakeside Trail in Augusta County, Virginia; BRP mileposts 47.5, 217.5, 230.1, 299.7, and 364.1; on the AT along Stover Creek in Georgia, Muskrat Creek Shelter in North Carolina, Laurel Fork Gorge in Tennessee, and Thunder Hill Shelter in central Virginia; and Riprap Trail in SNP.

SPOTTED WINTERGREEN

Chimaphila maculata

Because its white-striped leaves stay green throughout the year, Spotted Wintergreen adds a touch of color and cheer to an otherwise brown and gray forest floor during the colder months, and its genus name *Chimaphila* (pronounced Kye-MAF-fil-uh) reflects this. When combined, the Greek words *cheima* and *phileo* translate as "winter-loving."

One of its other common names, Pipsissewa, can lead to a great deal of confusion, because it is also applied to another species, *Chimaphila umbellata,* which, although growing a bit larger, has a very similar appearance and flowers. Its shining, dark green leaves have smaller teeth and lack the mottled appearance of the Spotted Wintergreen's white veins. To add to this befuddlement, other common names—such as Prince's Pine, Love-in-Winter, Bittersweet, King's Cure, Noble Pine, and Pine Tulip—have been applied to both species. In addition, these two plants should not be confused with Wintergreen (*Gaultheria procumbens*), a creeping plant with small, shiny, oval-shaped leaves and dangling, waxy, egg-shaped flowers that bloom from July to August.

Some authorities include Spotted Wintergreen in the Heath family, which includes Great Rhododendron (*Rhododendron maximum;* see page 64) and Mountain Laurel (*Kalmia latifolia;* see page 174). Others, such as Roger Tory Peterson, place it in the Wintergreen, or Pyrola, family. Spotted Wintergreen spreads by seeds and underground shoots and appears to benefit from minor forest fires, as studies have shown its numbers increase after them.

Some places you may encounter Spotted Wintergreen include: Jack Branch Trail in Madison County, and Hangover Lead South Trail in the Joyce Kilmer–Slickrock Wilderness in North Carolina; along most of the trails in Hungry Mother State Park in Virginia; BRP mileposts 55.1, 63.6, and 83.3; and upland forests of Catoctin Mountain Park in Maryland.

OXEYE DAISY
Chrysanthemum
leucanthemum

FLOWER:
The inner, flattened or depressed, yellow disk flowers are surrounded by fifteen to thirty-five outer, white ray petals.

LEAVES AND STEM:
The narrow, dark green sessile leaves are toothed or lobed and arranged alternately on a stem that rises one to three feet.

BLOOM SEASON:
June to August

The Daisy has had a long and colorful history in the Old World, where it is a native plant. In ancient Greece it was believed to be revered by the goddess Artemis, who was the daughter of Zeus, the thunder god. At times Artemis would ask her father to refrain from hurling lightning bolts earthward, and for this reason folklore referred to the Daisy as the Thunder Flower. Centuries later in Europe the plant came to be called Dun Flower, "Dun" being a Scandinavian word for thunder.

Herbalists prescribed various concoctions made from the Daisy to treat inflamed eyes, coughs, ruptures, broken ribs, burns, wounds, open sores, jaundice, menstrual pains, and more. The young leaves and white petals have been added to salads, and Daisy wine is said to be as refreshing as Dandelion wine.

The plant was a favorite of Chaucer's; he wrote about it often and called it "ee of the daie" and "day's eye," which is obviously where the common name comes from. The genus name is derived from the Greek words *chrysos*, meaning "gold," and *anthemom*, "flower." Although related, Oxeye Daisy is not a Chrysanthemum and it has now been classified as a different genus, which is why, when looking to other sources for further information, you should be aware that some reference books list it as *Leucanthemum vulgare*.

In his book *Hedgemaids and Fairy Candles*, Jack Sanders gives twenty common names for Oxeye Daisy, including Dutch Morgan, Moon Penny, Herb Margeret, Butter Daisy, Horse Gowan, Maudlinwort, and Poverty Weed.

Some places you may encounter Oxeye Daisy include: Cades Cove and Little River Road in GSMNP; Cherohala Skyway in North Carolina; BRP mileposts 78.4, 89, 162.4, 277.9, 308.2, and 409.4; fields of Sky Meadows State Park in Virginia; Woods Lock on the C&O Canal, and roadsides in Catoctin Mountain Park in Maryland.

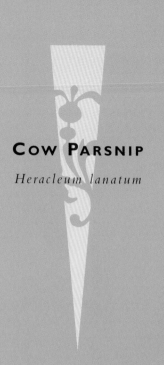

COW PARSNIP

Heracleum lanatum

Cow Parsnip is a native of North America and may be found in almost every state and in many provinces in Canada. Like its relative, Queen Anne's Lace (*Daucus carota;* see page 62), its flowers grow in an umbel, and those situated on the outside are larger than those in the middle. The five petals of each blossom are asymmetrical, with the smaller petals being notched and the larger ones being deeply lobed.

The genus name *Heracleum* honors the hero of classical Greek myths, Hercules, who valued the plant for its medicinal qualities. Indeed, Cow Parsnip, also known as Masterwort, has been used throughout the centuries to treat a variety of ailments, such as rheumatism and headaches. There are still some people who, despite the plant's offensive odor when crushed, enjoy eating its young stems, leaves, and roots. However, great care must be made to correctly identify the plant because the flowers and leaves of Poison Hemlock (*Conium maculatum*) and Water Hemlock (*Cicuta maculata*) resemble those of Cow Parsnip. Both Hemlocks are common throughout the Blue Ridge and Great Smoky Mountains, are highly toxic, and should be avoided. Poison Hemlock was the plant used to kill Socrates.

When looking to other sources for information about Cow Parsnip, you should be aware that some reference books classify it as *Heracleum maximum.*

Some places you may encounter Cow Parsnip include: BRP mileposts 425.9, 432.7, 435.2, and 440.8; along roads, stream banks, and open meadows in Botetourt County in Virginia; on the AT on the southern flank of Hazeltop Mountain; and at many trail crossings of Skyline Drive in SNP.

MICHAUX'S SAXIFRAGE

Saxifraga michauxii

FLOWER:

The quarter-inch, star-shaped white flowers have five petals: three larger petals that are heart-shaped at the base and have two yellow spots, and two smaller petals that have tapering bases and no spots.

LEAVES AND STEM:

Arranged in a basal rosette-like cluster, the leaves are three to seven inches long, have coarse, sharp teeth, and turn a rich red underneath and on the tips when mature.

BLOOM SEASON:

June to August

Many plants have flowers that are botanically classified as being radially symmetrical, meaning the petals (or petal-like parts) are arranged around a center like the spokes on a wheel, and each part is similar in shape, size, and spacing. The flowers of the Michaux's Saxifrage are bilaterally symmetrical in that the petals are dissimilar but arranged in such a way that they produce left and right mirror images.

Michaux's Saxifrage, also known as Mountain Saxifrage, inhabits the southern portion of the Blue Ridge and Great Smoky Mountains, growing from Virginia to Georgia. Other Saxifrages that may be found in the range include Early Saxifrage (*Saxifraga virginiensis*), which blooms in March and April, whose floral stalk is shorter and thicker, and whose flower petals lack the small yellow dots; and Lettuce Saxifrage (*Saxifraga micranthidifolia*), with flower stalks that grow one to three feet high. Both have flowers with five petals that are radially symmetrical. Brook Saxifrage (*Boykina aconitifolia*) has similar flowers, but its leaves are more expansive, five- to seven-lobed, and long-stalked.

The Saxifrages receive their name from their ability to grow in the crevices of rocky cliffs and among the rocks found on sunny slopes with moist seepage areas. People once believed that the plants caused the cracks and tiny fissures in which they are rooted—thus the Latin word for "stone," *saxum*, was combined with *fragere*, which means "to break."

Some places you may encounter one of the Saxifrages include: Balsam Mountain and Newfound Gap Roads, and Noland Divide and Kanati Fork Trails in GSMNP; BRP mileposts 63.6 and 86; and on the AT at Jennings Creek and on The Priest in central Virginia, and between Big Meadows Lodge and Skyland Lodge in SNP.

RATTLESNAKE PLANTAIN

Goodyera pubescens

FLOWER:
Growing in a dense cluster at the end of a six- to eighteen-inch hairy spike, the flowers of the Rattlesnake Plantain are so small (about a quarter inch in diameter) that you will need to get close to study them. Each tiny blossom has two petals and an upper sepal that cover a lower lip.

LEAVES AND STEM:
Appearing in a basal rosette, the broad leaves are bluish-green and marked by a network of white veins.

BLOOM SEASON:
Late June to August

Also known as Rattlesnake Orchid, the Rattlesnake Plantain is sometimes mistaken for the Rattlesnake Weed (*Hieracium venosum*), and vice versa, because they both have similar-looking basal leaves. The telling difference is that the Rattlesnake Weed has reddish-purple leaf veins, whereas the Rattlesnake Plantain's leaves are white-veined. In addition, the latter has stalks of tiny white flowers, easily distinguished from the Rattlesnake Weed's blossoms (which look like little yellow Dandelions).

The leaves of both plants gave them their common names, as the vein patterns resemble the markings on a rattlesnake. Supporting this name is the fact that the Rattlesnake Plantain's fruit cluster rattles slightly when shaken.

Folklorists have not been able to find the origin of the belief, but some Native American women rubbed the plant against their bodies because it was supposed to make their husbands fall more deeply in love with them.

Another Rattlesnake Plantain that inhabits the Blue Ridge and Great Smoky Mountains is the Dwarf Rattlesnake Plantain (*Goodyera repens*). A shorter plant that rarely reaches more than ten inches in height, its blossoms are smaller and only grow on one side of the floral spike. Although members of the Orchid family, not of the Plantain, the Rattlesnake Plantains were given their common names because their leaves grow in basal rosettes, like those of true Plantains.

Some places you may encounter one of the Rattlesnake Plantains include: Balsam Mountain Road, and Porters Creek and Cosby Nature Trails in GSMNP; Hangover Lead South Trail in Joyce Kilmer–Slickrock Wilderness in North Carolina; on the AT between Timber Ridge Trail and Albert Mountain in North Carolina, and close to Bryant Ridge Shelter and along Thunder Ridge in central Virginia.

75

INDIAN PIPE

Monotropa uniflora

Indian Pipe, an odd-looking but certainly enchanting plant, is the subject of a Cherokee legend. The Great Spirit of the Cherokees once found the leaders of the tribe's seven clans smoking the peace pipe before they had actually reached an agreement on an important matter. Outraged, he killed the members of this perfidious gathering, and Indian Pipe now grows as a reminder of their serious breach of rules.

Favoring the moist, rich soil of a heavily shaded forest, Indian Pipe is most often found growing in small clusters and certainly does not fit our usual image of a wildflower. Because it lacks chlorophyll (the substance that gives plants their green color and enables them to obtain nourishment from the sun), it has a translucent appearance and is often mistaken for a fungus. Yet, like other flowers, it produces nectar and pollen and is fertilized by visiting insects.

Indian Pipe's long blooming season sometimes lasts into late September, but each individual plant blooms for just a short while. Surviving most of the year underground, the plant does not send up a shoot until it is ready to bloom, and once it has become fertilized and produced seeds, its aboveground part turns black, wilts, and disappears.

Pinesap (*Monotropa hypopithys*) is similar to Indian Pipe but is reddish-yellow and has several nodding flowers per stem. Sweet Pinesap (*Monotropsis odorata*) is much smaller, often hidden under forest litter, and very fragrant.

Some places you may encounter Indian Pipe include: Van Cliff Trail in Madison County and Hangover Lead South Trail in Joyce Kilmer–Slickrock Wilderness in North Carolina; Rich Mountain Road, and Spruce-Fir Nature and Cooper Road Trails in GSMNP; on the AT between Cheoah Bald and Stecoah Gap in North Carolina, and Catawba Mountain in central Virginia; Freer Trail in Blackwater Creek Natural Area in Lynchburg, Virginia; and Rose River Fire Road in SNP.

BROADLEAF
MEADOWSWEET

Spiraea latifolia

FLOWER:
The quarter-inch white to pale pink flowers grow in dense terminal clusters and have five white petals, five sepals, (usually) five pistils, and an abundance of stamens.

LEAVES AND STEM:
The one- to three-inch leaves are coarsely toothed and lanceolate in shape but may be a bit broader above their middle portion.

BLOOM SEASON:
June to September

Favoring stream banks, moist fields, and swampy areas, Broadleaf Meadowsweet is a woody shrub that inhabits all but the most southern portion of the Blue Ridge and Great Smoky Mountains. It is a member of the Rose family, which includes thousands of species worldwide, among them Apples, Pears, Cherries, Peaches, Apricots, Blackberries, Raspberries, Hawthorns, Mountain Ash, Wild Strawberries (*Fragaria virginiana;* see page 38), and Goatsbeard (*Aruncus dioicus;* see page 56).

Growing as tall as five feet, but usually in the two- to three-foot range, the Broadleaf Meadowsweet's twigs are a reddish-brown and hairless. The fruit's small, dry pods stay on the plant long after the flowers have faded and fallen, and the leaves drop off in the fall. Narrowleaf Meadowsweet (*Spiraea alba*) has yellowish-brown twigs that are hairy, and its leaves are narrower and more lanceolate. The leaves of the Virginia Spiraea (*Spiraea virginia*) are broadest near the tip, and its flower clusters are flatter.

A tea made from Meadowsweet leaves was said to be a restorative, yet André Michaux, for whom the Michaux's Saxifrage (*Saxifraga michauxii;* see page 72) is named, claimed that Native Americans called the plant *papiconah* and used it as a purgative.

The ancient Greeks made wreaths and garlands from the flexible branches, and it is believed that the genus name is derived from their word *speiros,* which means "a spiral." Later in history, the British employed Spiraea wreaths in weddings, and the plants came to be known as Bridewort and Bridal Wreath.

Some places you may encounter one of the Meadowsweets include: BRP milepost 230.1 and Fenwick Mines Wetlands Trail in Craig County, Virginia.

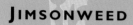

JIMSONWEED

Datura stramonium

FLOWER:
The (usually) three- to four-inch, five-lobed, trumpet-shaped flowers are most often white with tinges of purple accenting them.

LEAVES AND STEM:
The three- to eight-inch leaves are irregularly toothed and grow alternately on the strong, forking, and branched stem that may be as much as five feet tall.

BLOOM SEASON:
June to September (or early October)

Growing up to five feet tall in fields, waste areas, and roadsides, Jimsonweed is not a shy, tiny plant, but one that loudly proclaims its presence with large, trumpet-shaped flowers. And well it should—for this is a plant to be avoided, as all parts of it are poisonous.

Just touching the leaves or flowers can cause a severe skin reaction in some people; grazing livestock have died from consuming small amounts.

The common name is a corruption of "Jamestown"; the plant was discovered growing close to this early English colony in America. It is also where the psychedelic effects of the prickly, egg-shaped fruit were discovered. British soldiers, marching to suppress an uprising by the colonists, found themselves running out of food and so ate the fruit. Within a few hours, the entire group was disoriented and hallucinating. Quite a number of people died in the 1960s and 1970s when they ingested the fruit in an attempt to cheaply replicate the effects of LSD. Others became extremely ill from smoking the dried leaves and flowers.

Native Americans, however, found that heating the leaves and then applying them to the skin would alleviate the pain of burns, and early settlers mixed animal fat with the cooked root and leaves to use as a poultice for the same purpose.

Related to tomatoes, Jimsonweed is a member of the Nightshade family and has other common names including Thorn Apple, Stramonium, and Devil's Trumpet.

Some places you may encounter Jimsonweed include: NC 28 south of Fontana Dam, and Bridal Veil Falls on NC 28 between Franklin and Highlands, North Carolina; BRP mileposts 78.4 and 95.4; and along US 460/US 22 in Botetourt County, and in the open areas of Sky Meadows State Park, Virginia.

FLOWERING SPURGE

Euphorbia corollata

Flowering Spurge. Rue Anemone (*Thalictrum thalictroides;* see page 12). Wood Anemone (*Anemone quinquefolia;* see page 24). Sharp-Lobed Hepatica (*Hepatica acutiloba;* see page 150). Pokeweed (*Phytolacca americana;* see page 84). Bunchberry. Dogwood. Poinsettia. All these plants have something in common. They have flowers with what appear to be petals but are actually leaf bracts, sepals, or some other petal-like appendages.

The five white "petals" of the Flowering Spurge are lobes on the rim of the involucre (a cup-shaped circle of bracts). At the base of each lobe is a yellowish-green gland that could be mistaken for a stamen. Within each involucre are several minute male flowers and one tiny female flower.

Several references state that the plant received its scientific name *Euphorbia* because Pliny, the famous Roman naturalist, once related the story that King Jubas of Mauritania named it for his favorite doctor, Euphorbus, and Pliny accepted what the King called it.

Like all members of the Spurge family, Flowering Spurge contains a milky juice that can be a powerful cathartic, and Native Americans used the plant to induce vomiting and diarrhea. In fact, their word for the plant was *peheca*, meaning "move (or act) quickly." The common name comes from the Latin word *purgare* and reflects the Spurge's ability to purge poisons from the body. However, it is such a powerful emetic that care had to be taken not to overdose the patient to the point that dehydration, and possibly death, would ensue.

Some places you may encounter Flowering Spurge include: dry, open areas in GSMNP; BRP mileposts 85.7–85.9, 252.8, 277.9, 388.8, and 438.9; on the AT near Whitetop Mountain and Buzzard Rock in southern Virginia; and South River Falls Trail, and Hawksbill Mountain in SNP.

POKEWEED

Phytolacca americana

FLOWER:
Growing in racemes that often emanate from the stem opposite one of the leaves, the flowers are only a quarter inch in size and have five petal-like white sepals.

LEAVES AND STEM:
The lance-shaped leaves are five to twelve inches long and the entire plant may reach a height of ten feet.

BLOOM SEASON:
July to September

If you grew up in the country, or even close to an abandoned lot in the city, you are probably familiar with this tall plant with its twelve-inch-long leaves and thick, purple stem. It is a good bet that you were attracted to its dark violet berries that begin to appear in midsummer. You found out that the juice from these berries made a great ink with which to stain your hands and clothes—sometimes indelibly. Luckily, you did not eat any, as their seeds are poisonous.

However, the young shoots are edible and have long been considered somewhat of a spring treat and delicacy by Native Americans, early settlers, and, unto this day, the Pennsylvania Dutch and many rural families. After a winter without fresh greens, the plant supplies an abundance of vitamins A and C.

Pokeweed also has a long history as a medicinal plant. The Delaware Indians used the roots in a liniment to reduce swelling and ate mashed roots as a blood purifier, while the Pamunkey boiled the berries into a concoction for rheumatism, and herbalists once mixed the plant's juices with gunpowder as a treatment for cancer. As is so often the case in folk medicine, there may have been some scientific basis for the latter use. Modern researchers have found Pokeweed to contain a mitogenic agent (a substance that initiates the division of cells) that may one day be used in cancer therapies.

The genus name is derived from the Greek *phytos,* meaning "plant," and the Italian *lacca,* for "red." When looking to other sources for information on Pokeweed, you should be aware that some reference books list it as *Phytolacca decandra.*

Some places you may encounter Pokeweed include: lower elevations of GSMNP; BRP mileposts 6, 74.7, 151, 239.9, 323, and 376.9; Ivy Creek Natural Area in Albemarle County in Virginia; Rockytop Trail in SNP; and roads in Catoctin Mountain Park in Maryland.

PALE INDIAN PLANTAIN

Cacalia atriplicifolia

Pale Indian Plantain favors dry open woods, roadsides, and meadows. It is a far-ranging plant that can be found not only in the Blue Ridge and Great Smoky Mountains but also in the tallgrass prairie regions of Illinois and Nebraska, as far north as Minnesota, and south into the Ozark Mountains of Arkansas.

As is the case with all wildflowers, one must accept that there are no hard and fast rules when it comes to bloom season. Although most references note that Pale Indian Plantain blooms from July to September, in some locales and years it may flower from June into October.

When looking to other sources for information on Pale Indian Plantain, you should be aware that some reference books list it as *Arnoglossum atriplicifolium*.

A relative, Great Indian Plantain (*Cacalia muhlenbergii*), is similar in appearance but has a heavily grooved stem that is purplish-red in color and can reach a height of nine feet. The leaves are more rounded and not waxy. Sweet-Scented Indian Plantain (*Cacalia suaveolens*) has arrowhead-shaped leaves with clearly defined, sharp teeth along the margins. Rugel's Indian Plantain (*Cacalia rugelia*) is believed to grow only in the higher elevations of the Great Smoky Mountains. Looking unlike the other Indian Plantains, it rarely attains a height of more than a foot, and its flower heads either nod or grow parallel to the ground.

Some places you may encounter one of the Indian Plantains include: Spruce-Fir Nature Trail, Mount LeConte, and Clingmans Dome in GSMNP; BRP milepost 235; and along Skyline Drive in SNP.

VIRGIN'S BOWER

Clematis virginiana

Introduced climbing vines, such as Honeysuckle and Kudzu, are often looked upon with disdain and viewed as nuisances and even threats. Yet, the native Virgin's Bower, which creeps across rocks and stone walls and clambers over shrubs and low trees has, in some people's opinion, so many redeeming values that it has been the recipient of a number of genial common names.

By using twisting leaf stems to attach itself to other plants and objects, it forms a heavy drapery of vines and foliage along roads, creating a cool spot to rest in the shade, or a shelter in which to escape a sudden rain shower, thereby earning it the name Traveler's Joy. The long, twisting, woolly gray plumes that are a part of its achenes (dry, one-seeded fruits that do not split open upon maturity) reminded some observers of their grandfather's whiskers, and they called it Old Man's Beard.

Although she did not assign a new name to the Virgin's Bower, Jean Hersey was so taken by the fragrance of its blossoms that in her book *The Woman's Day Book of Wildflowers* she describes it as "new-mown hay in sunlight." This is certainly a smell all of us have experienced at one time or another and one that conjures images of lazy summer days spent roaming an idyllic countryside.

Of course, not everyone has such a kind opinion of this plant. Those trying to keep fields, meadows, and border areas from becoming overgrown have dubbed it the Devil's Darning Needle. Other common names include Gander Vine, Wild Hops, and Common Clematis.

Some places you may encounter Virgin's Bower include: Cades Cove and around the Oconaluftee Visitor Center in GSMNP; BRP mileposts 13.1, 85.8, 176.1, 285–289, 289.8, and 313–314; and in the higher elevations of Catoctin Mountain Park in Maryland.

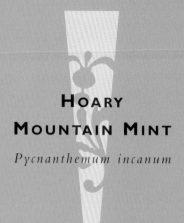

HOARY MOUNTAIN MINT

Pycnanthemum incanum

FLOWER:
  The small, white to bluish-purple blossoms grow in clusters at the top of the stem and from the axils of the upper leaves. Each flower is less than a half inch long and has two lips, the lower one having purple spots.

LEAVES AND STEM:
  The one- to four-inch leaves are broadly lanceolate, toothed, white underneath, and stalked, and they grow oppositely on the one- to three-foot hairy stem. The upper leaves, like the flower, are covered in fine, white hairs.

BLOOM SEASON:
  July to September

It can be hard for anyone other than a truly dedicated wildflower enthusiast to name or differentiate among the multitude of Mints found in the eastern part of the United States. Yet, there can be no mistaking the Hoary Mountain Mint. So many fine, white hairs (thus, the name hoary) grow upon the leaves and bracts just below the flower clusters that they appear to have a layer of powdery dust on them. This is so visible that when the plant grows in large colonies it can give the forest understory a patina of white, a phenomenon that has earned it another common name, Snow on the Mountain.

The genus name *Pycnanthemum* is a reference to its tight cluster of flowers, and comes from the Greek words *pucnos,* meaning "dense," and *anthemum,* for "flower."

Among the many other Mints to be found in the Blue Ridge and Great Smoky Mountains are Horse Balm (*Collinsonia canadensis;* see page 146), Bee Balm (*Monarda didyma;* see page 196), Heal-All (*Prunella vulgaris;* see page 218), Wild Bergamot (*Monarda fistulosa;* see page 186), and Wild Basil (*Satureja vulgaris;* see page 188). If the aroma and flowers of a plant are not enough to help you positively identify it as a Mint, just run your fingers up and down its main stem. Almost all Mints have square stems, a rare trait.

Some places you may encounter one of the Mints include: Little River Trail and Balsam Mountain Road in GSMNP; BRP milepost 248, 277.9, 411, and 432.7; on the AT between Tray and Rocky Mountains in Georgia, and south of McAfee Knob in central Virginia; Turkey Roost Trail at Lake Robertson near Lexington, Virginia; and the woods roads of Sugarloaf Mountain, and the C&O Canal in Frederick County, Maryland.

GRASS-OF-PARNASSUS

Parnassia asarifolia

FLOWER:

The inch-wide flower, which grows atop its own six- to twenty-inch stalk, has five broadly oval, white petals beautifully accented by prominent green veins.

LEAVES AND STEM:

The two- to four-inch basal leaves are on long stalks and are kidney shaped. One nearly rounded leaf clasps and grows about halfway up the flower stem.

BLOOM SEASON:

July to October

Grass-of-Parnassus is certainly one of the prettiest and most distinctive-looking five-petaled, star-shaped white flowers to be found in the Blue Ridge and Great Smoky Mountains. Each petal is prominently marked by eleven to fifteen green radiating principal veins. Forming a circle around the pistil is a group of three-pronged staminodia, or sterile stamens, that are just a bit shorter than the fertile stamens that are tipped by yellow anthers. The resemblance of the kidney-shaped basal leaves to those of the Wild Ginger (*Asarum canadense;* see page 246) is indicated by the species name *asarifolia.* What makes the plant all the more special is that it is not very common, as it is confined to the few moist and rocky areas in the higher elevations of the region.

An even rarer species, Large-Leaf-Grass-of-Parnassus (*Parnassia grandifolia*) has oblong to ovate leaves, and flowers that are one-and-a-half to two inches across with fewer veins on each petal and slender staminodia that are longer than the stamens.

Despite the common name, neither the leaves nor the flower resemble those of the grasses. An old story says that Dioscorides, a noted naturalist who lived during the first century A.D., discovered a similar plant growing on Parnassus, a mountain in Greece sacred to Apollo. Scholars theorize that in naming the flower he mistook the meadow's grasses to be a part of the plant's foliage.

Some places you may encounter Grass-of-Parnassus include: Yellow Mountain Trail in Jackson County, North Carolina; and Mount LeConte in GSMNP.

WHITE SNAKEROOT

Eupatorium rugosum

White Snakeroot grows so abundantly throughout the Blue Ridge and Great Smoky Mountains—and is such an innocent-looking plant—that it may be hard to believe that it was once the leading cause of death from disease in the United States.

Throughout the 1800s and into the early part of the twentieth century, a mysterious ailment killed thousands of people, including Abraham Lincoln's mother, Nancy Hanks Lincoln. Many things were blamed for the deaths, including bacteria, poison ivy, and even mysterious "vapors rising from the earth." So feared was the disease that everyone deserted the community when the sickness first appeared. It was not until 1917 that researchers discovered White Snakeroot to be the source of the disease, which has come to be called "milk sickness." The plant contains a toxic compound, tremetol, that tainted the milk of grazing livestock and was passed on to the humans who drank it. Although cattle may still occasionally eat White Snakeroot, the commercial processing of milk mixes so many different sources that the toxin becomes diluted.

When looking to other sources for information on White Snakeroot, you should be aware that some reference books list it as *Eupatorium urticaefolium* or *Ageratina altissima*.

Smaller White Snakeroot (*Eupatorium aromaticum* or *Ageratina aromatica*) has smaller, thicker leaves that are shiny on top and clusters that contain fewer flowers. Despite the name, this species has no aroma.

Some places you may encounter White Snakeroot include: Balsam Mountain Nature and Clingmans Dome Trails in GSMNP; BRP mileposts 235, 242.3, 272, 289.6, 303.7, 431, 451.2, and 457.9; higher elevations of Mount Mitchell in North Carolina; Lovingston Springs Trail in Amherst County, Virginia; and in the lower elevations of Catoctin Mountain Park in Maryland.

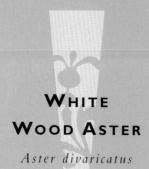

WHITE WOOD ASTER

Aster divaricatus

The one-inch flower heads grow atop (often) zigzagging stems and have six to ten white rays, disk flowers that start out yellow and often turn brown, and whitish leaf bracts tipped green.

The leaves, which are heart-shaped closer to the bottom and more lanceolate near the top, can be two to seven inches long, with the lower ones being more sharply toothed than the upper ones.

July to October

The Asters can be a confusing lot. There are thought to be more than several hundred of them worldwide, with only subtle differences, such as leaf shape or the number of rays, distinguishing one from the other. Some are purple and some are white. Those that grow in the fields tend to have narrow leaves and an abundance of rays, while those found in the forest usually have larger leaves and fewer rays. Some appear fairly early in the blooming season; others persist well into fall, disappearing only after frost. Don't be too hard on yourself if you have trouble identifying a particular species. Even Asa Gray, the author of the well-respected and oft-consulted *Manual of Botany*, became frustrated and exclaimed, "Never was there so rascally a genus; they reduce me to despair!"

An old myth tells of the origin of the Asters. One day the goddess of justice, Virgo (also known as Astraes), who was the daughter of Jupiter and Themses, gazed upon the earth and was saddened to find that there were no stars. Where her tears fell, Asters began to grow.

Among the many other Asters in the region are the Big-Leaved Aster (*Aster macrophyllus*), with wide basal leaves and bluish-purple (sometimes white) rays, and the Mountain Wood Aster (*Aster chlorolepis*), which has ten or more ray flowers and is usually found only in higher elevations.

Some places you may encounter White Wood Aster include: School House Gap Trail and Clingmans Dome Road in GSMNP; BRP mileposts 154.1, 168, 179.3, 189.1, 218.7, 252.8, 260.3, 272, 289.6, 290.5, 301.8, 303.7, 306.6, 308.2, 350.4, 359.9, 364.5, 399.7, 409.4, 411, 421.7, 432.7, 446, 453.4, and 467.8; and on the AT north of Newfound Gap in GSMNP.

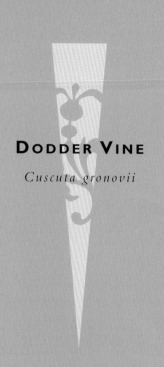

DODDER VINE

Cuscuta gronovii

FLOWER:
  The small (eighth-inch), bell-shaped, five-lobed flowers grow in tight clusters along the orangish-yellow vine.

LEAVES AND STEM:
  Leaves are basically absent, being reduced to small scales upon the twisting vine.

BLOOM SEASON:
  August to October

The life of the Dodder Vine reads like a horror story. A mysterious seed is carried to a faraway place by an unsuspecting bird, animal, or person, where it falls to the ground and germinates. Taking root, it sends up a shoot that develops into a climbing vine that twists itself in tight coils around other plants. Containing no chlorophyll or leaves from which to produce food from sunlight, it sends out suckers that penetrate the flesh of its host plant, robbing its benefactor of needed nourishment. From here, it climbs onto additional plants, creating a tangle many feet long. Eventually, the roots and lower portions of the vine dry up and die, as it now parasitizes everything it needs from the other plants.

The vine is named for Johan (or Jan) Fredrik (or Frederich) Gronovius, the author of *Flora Virginica,* published in the mid-1700s. In applying this species name, Linnaeus bestowed something of a backhanded honor, for he considered Gronovius to be overly ambitious and stated that *Cuscuta gronovii* was "a climbing plant which grasps all other plants."

Thriving primarily in moist areas of low ground, there are a number of other species of Dodder Vines found in the Blue Ridge and Great Smoky Mountains, but it is difficult to tell one from the other. *Cuscuta gronovii,* which has other common names such as Common Dodder, Love Vine, and Love-in-a-Tangle, grows on a variety of host plants, while Beaked Dodder (*Cuscuta rostrata*) is almost always found twisted around Blackberry bushes.

Some places you may encounter one of the Dodder Vines include: Cades Cove Loop Road and Kanati Fork Trail in GSMNP; and BRP mileposts 303.7 and 304.7.

NODDING
LADIES' TRESSES

Spiranthes cernua

FLOWER:
Growing in a spiral arrangement along a spike that may reach twenty-four inches are half-inch white flowers that nod toward the ground. It takes a close look to appreciate their true beauty. Two side petals merge with an upper sepal to form a hood over the lower, wavy-lipped petal.

LEAVES AND STEM:
The basal leaves are long (up to ten inches), slender, and almost grasslike. The upper leaves are not much more than scales.

BLOOM SEASON:
August to October (or first frost)

For those who admire and study orchids, it seems that members of this family almost always have ingenious and interesting methods of becoming fertilized, and the Nodding Ladies' Tresses are no exceptions.

When a new flower develops, the first insect to visit it (which in the case of the Nodding Ladies' Tresses will probably be a bumblebee) breaks apart a small fascia that releases a glue, thereby insuring that any pollen that comes in contact with the insect will stick to it and travel on to the next flower.

Charles Darwin was one of the first to observe that the insects almost always work their way from the bottom to the top blossoms along the plants' flower spikes. No sure reason for this behavior has been established. However, because the flowers mature from bottom to top, those on the bottom will be the ones most ready to be fertilized by the pollen the insect has picked up from visiting a previous flower spike. Fertilization is aided by the fact that as the flower matures, the opening in the fascia continues to get wider, providing the insect with easy access to the stigma inside.

Spiranthes is from the Greek *spirea,* for "spiral," and *anthos,* meaning "flower," and describes the way the blossoms grow along the spike. "Nodding," of course, refers to the way the flowers point toward the ground, and "tress" is a word once used to describe braided hair.

Because they both have spikes of white flowers, Nodding Ladies' Tresses might be confused with the Rattlesnake Plantain (*Goodyera pubescens;* see page 74), but the latter has broad, heavily veined basal leaves.

Some places you may encounter Nodding Ladies' Tresses include: Chattahoochee Nature Center in Roswell, Georgia; Forney Ridge Trail, Cades Cove, and Laurel Falls Trail in GSMNP; BRP mileposts 303.7 and 365–368; and on the AT near Punchbowl Shelter in central Virginia.

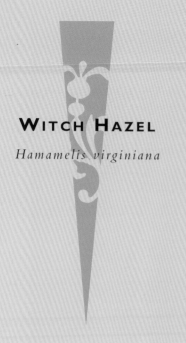

WITCH HAZEL

Hamamelis virginiana

FLOWER:
The four petals of the one-inch flowers have been likened to spider legs or crinkly ribbon as they spread outward from the leafless branches of the shrub.

LEAVES AND STEM:
The three- to six-inch leaves have wavy edges, are broadly ovate, turn a brilliant yellow in autumn, and will have fallen off the branches before the flowers appear. The shrub is usually no more than ten feet high but can reach a height of close to thirty feet.

BLOOM SEASON:
September to January

The question is: Are the Witch Hazel's flowers the last of the season's blossoms, or are they the first ones to greet the promise of a new year? Since the shrub can be in bloom from early autumn into January, and its flowers may range from a yellowish-white to a deep yellow, it has been placed in this book at the end of the white flowers' blooming season and the beginning of the yellow flowers' section. We leave it up to you to decide if it is the year's alpha or omega.

At about the same time the flowers first appear, the seedpods from last year's blossoms begin to break open. If you happen to be in the woods on the day that the temperature and humidity are just right, you may feel like you have stepped into a woodland war zone, as the pods open with a pop and send seeds arcing ten to twenty feet into the air.

Witch Hazel oil, made primarily from the leaves (but which can also be distilled from the bark, twigs, and roots), has a long history of medicinal use and can still be found in most pharmacies. An astringent, it is used to treat burns, boils, wounds, and hemorrhoids. As a gargle, it is said to relieve the pain of sore throats, and medical books of the 1800s recommended it for diarrhea. Some modern herbal books say two to three cups of Witch Hazel tea will help varicose veins.

Some places you are likely to encounter Witch Hazel include: Yellow Creek Mountain Trail in Graham County, North Carolina; Little River Gorge and close to the Bud Ogle Trailhead in GSMNP; BRP mileposts 19, 130.5, 293.2, 295.4, 305.1, 308.3, 339.5, 347.6, and 367.7; and Laurel Run Trail in Rockbridge County, Virginia.

TROUT LILY

Erythronium americanum

The Trout Lily is one of the first wildflowers to push its way through the soil in early spring, and it closes up each night to protect its inner parts from the still-cool air and chilly winds. As dawn's sunlight creeps across the mountainsides, the petals and sepals begin to move, eventually curving backward to greet the day.

The Trout Lily's seeds develop small corms, which, after being on the ground for a full year, send out runners (or droppers as some botanists call them) deep into the soil and close to a foot away from the seed. Supplied nutrients through this small strand, a new corm soon develops. In this way, a single seed can produce about ten new plants in the space of just a few years, and this is why you almost always see not just one plant, but a large colony. These colonies, some of which have been found to be more than a hundred years old, have a large network of deep roots that helps prevent erosion and stabilize the soil so that other plants may grow.

Queen bees feast on the Trout Lily's nectar and pollen, which is carried back to the nest to feed growing broods. In turn, these bees fan out into fields and forests, gathering pollen and nectar and fertilizing countless other plants.

Other common names include Fawn Lily, Dogtooth Violet, and Adder's Tongue.

Some places you may encounter Trout Lily include: Sosebee Cove in Union County, Georgia; Cove Hardwood Nature and Roaring Fork Motor Nature Trails in GSMNP; BRP milepost 162.4; on the AT between Deep Gap and Wallace Gap, and close to Walnut Mountain Shelter in North Carolina, north of VA 624 in central Virginia, and in low areas throughout SNP; and in the lower elevations of Catoctin Mountain Park in Maryland.

FLOWER:
The nodding, one-and-a-half-inch, yellow flower has six petals and sepals that bend in a graceful, backward curve.

LEAVES AND STEM:
The four- to six-inch elliptical leaves are mottled purple-brown and grow near the base of the six- to nine-inch stem.

BLOOM SEASON:
March to May

COMMON CINQUEFOIL

Potentilla simplex

FLOWER:

Rising on a single stem and looking somewhat like a small Rose, the light-yellow Common Cinquefoil flower has five petals and five large sepals. Some observers feel that the flower resembles those of the Wild Strawberry (Fragaria virginiana; see page 38).

LEAVES AND STEM:

The leaves of the Common Cinquefoil are divided into five radiating leaflets that are noticeably toothed. Each one rises on its own stalk from the hairy, horizontal runners.

BLOOM SEASON:

April to June

The word cinquefoil in this plant's name comes from the French *cinque,* for "five," and *foil,* for "foliage" or "parts." Indeed, much about the plant comes in fives: the flower has five petals and five sepals, and the leaf is divided into five leaflets.

The genus name *Potentilla* comes from the Middle Ages when it was believed that the numerous species had potent properties as medicinal plants. It was used to treat mouth sores, stomach ulcers, diarrhea, nosebleeds, and more. Some species contain large amounts of tannin, enabling them to be used as an astringent and in the tanning of leather. Today, members of the genus are the source of a drug used to relieve muscle spasms.

Other Cinquefoils that grow in the Blue Ridge and Great Smoky Mountains include Canadian Dwarf Cinquefoil (*Potentilla canadensis*), which is similar in appearance but has smaller leaves that are only toothed along their upper half. Its berries were a favorite treat of Henry David Thoreau. An import from Europe, Rough-Fruited Cinquefoil (*Potentilla recta*) is one of the largest of the genus, with pale-yellow, one-and-a-half-inch flowers that grow in a terminal cluster on a one- to two-foot-high stem. The leaves of Silvery Cinquefoil (*Potentilla argentea*) are shaped somewhat like those of the oak tree and are silvery-white underneath.

Some places you may encounter one of the Cinquefoils include: Rich Mountain and Fightin' Creek Gap Roads, and Kanati Fork Trail in GSMNP; BRP mileposts 17.6, 78.4, 110.9, 235, 399.7, and 460.8; on the AT on Wayah Bald in North Carolina, and Rice Field and Symms Gap in central Virginia; Big Meadows in SNP; and along roads in Catoctin Mountain Park in Maryland.

SQUAWROOT

Conopholis americana

The half-inch yellowish to tan flowers have two lips, with the upper one forming a hood over a three-lobed, spreading lower lip.

Unconventional looking, the tannish-yellow leaves of Squawroot are scalelike and crowded tightly along a fleshy-looking stalk three to nine inches tall.

April to June

Squawroot's odd look has people often mistaking it for a mushroom or some other type of fungus. However, it is a member of the Broomrape family, which are low-growing, fleshy herbaceous plants that, lacking chlorophyll, obtain nourishment as parasites on other plants. The family name indicates that some of the species are parasites on shrubs that are members of the Pea family, commonly known as Brooms.

You may have to get down on your knees to really appreciate the minute parts of this plant that is a favorite springtime food of black bears. Each half-inch flower is protected by a scalelike leaf bract; protruding beyond the lower lip of the three fused petals are four stamens so small that you may need a magnifying glass to see them.

Another common name for Squawroot is Cancer Root, but don't confuse Squawroot with other parasitic plants of the same name, such as One-Flowered Cancer Root (*Orobanche uniflora;* see page 254) or Yellow Cancer Root (*Orobanche fasciculata*)—which more closely resemble Indian Pipe (*Monotropa uniflora;* see page 76). To confuse things even further, Black Cohosh (*Cimicifuga racemosa*) is sometimes referred to as Squawroot because it too was employed by Native Americans to alleviate the pains of menstruation.

Some places you may encounter Squawroot include: The Pocket on Pigeon Mountain in Walker County, Georgia; Rich Mountain Road and Laurel Falls Trail in GSMNP; BRP mileposts 260.3 and 403.8; on the AT at Chattahoochee Gap in Georgia, south of Deep Gap in North Carolina, and south of Scorched Earth Gap in central Virginia; Comers Creek Falls Trail in Smyth County, Virginia; and Maryland Heights Trail in Maryland, across the Potomac River from Harpers Ferry, West Virginia.

GOLDEN RAGWORT

Senecio aureus

Growing in flat-topped terminal clusters, the Daisy-like flowerheads are less than one inch across and have eight to twelve bright yellow rays.

Growing on a stem of one to three feet in height, the one- to six-inch basal leaves are heart-shaped with a bit of red underneath, while the upper leaves are narrower and only one to four inches long.

April to July

Looking more like the Daisies of late summer and fall, Golden Ragwort is a flower of spring and early summer. Despite the beauty it provides by adding splashes of sunshine yellow to wet meadows, moist woods, and swampy areas, the plant should be avoided as it is considered a highly toxic plant. Yet, in the past it was known as Squaw-Weed because Native Americans and early settlers used the root and leaves to make a tea for menstrual irregularities and complications of childbirth. It was also believed to help relieve the pains of difficult urination.

The species name of *Senecio* is Latin for "old man" and refers to the fluffy white material found on mature seeds that reminded some people of an old person's beard.

When looking to other sources for further information on Golden Ragwort, you should be aware some reference books list it as *Packera aurea*.

Roundleaf, or Spatulate-Leaved, Ragwort (*Senecio obovatus*) grows only one to one-and-a-half feet tall and has one- to three-inch, spoon-shaped basal leaves. The flowerheads of Yellow Ragwort (*Senecio anonymus*) are less than one-half inch across, and the basal leaves are elliptical with long stalks, while the upper ones become progressively smaller, stalkless, and cut into many segments. Rugel's Ragwort (*Rugelia nudicaulis*), also known as Rugel's Indian Plantain (*Cacalia rugelia*), is found only in the Great Smoky Mountains National Park. Growing at higher elevations, it has nodding blossoms with bracts that surround the small protruding disk flowers.

Some places you may encounter one of the Ragworts include: Cades Cove Loop and Clingmans Dome Roads, and The Boulevard, Spruce-Fir Nature, and Schoolhouse Gap Trails in GSMNP; and BRP mileposts 17.6, 38.8, 55.1, 63.6, 189.1, 242.3, 252.8, 272, 301.8, 326, 350.4, 380, 441, 448.1, and 460.8.

YELLOW
LADY'S SLIPPER

Cypripedium calceolus

The upper two petals are long and slender and range from yellow-green to purple-brown. It is the other petal, though, that makes this plant so distinctive. It is one to two inches long, bulbous in shape, and richly yellow and folds to a deep cleft in the middle.

The four- to eight-inch leaves are parallel-veined and grow alternately on a stem that may reach more than two feet in height.

April to June

Just looking at the shape of the Yellow Lady's Slipper blossom makes it easy to understand how it received the species name *calceolus*, which is Latin for "little shoe." In addition, the genus name *Cypripedium* is from the Greek language and translates—depending on which source you consult—as "sock" or "Venus's shoe."

Although many of us would have a hard time telling them apart, botanists recognize two variations of the Yellow Lady's Slipper. The flower pouch of the Small Yellow Lady's Slipper (*Cypripedium calceolus* var. *parviflorum*) is only about an inch in size, while the Large Lady's Slipper (*Cypripedium calceolus* var. *pubescens*) has a larger pouch, and its other petals are less twisted.

Also found in the region, the Pink Lady's Slipper (*Cypripedium acaule;* see page 254) grows as a single flower atop a long stem that emanates from two Lily-like leaves. Although it is rarely seen, the Showy Lady's Slipper (*Cypripedium reginae*) is the largest of the Lady's Slippers. Its petals and sepals are a pure white, while the pouch is tinged with a pinkish-rose hue. The pouch is also marked with dots or lines of deep magenta.

The admonishment not to pick any wildflowers is even stronger with the Lady's Slippers, as they appear to become rarer every year. Although it has been publicized for years that the plants will almost certainly not survive being transplanted, unthinking—or maybe uncaring—people continue to dig them up. Because of this problem, and in the hope that the plant will continue to be found throughout the region, it was decided not to include in this book specific sites where you might encounter Lady's Slippers in the Blue Ridge and Great Smoky Mountains.

YELLOW
STAR GRASS

Hypoxis hirsuta

FLOWER:
The six-parted, three-quarter-inch, bright-yellow flowers grow in clusters of two or more on slender stalks from two to six inches long. Each flower has six stamens, and three petals and three sepals that look identical.

LEAVES AND STEM:
The one-quarter-inch-wide leaves look like blades of grass and grow to about twelve inches.

BLOOM SEASON:
April to September

Although it is listed as blooming from April to September, Yellow Star Grass may not be in flower for the entire period in any one location—a shame, for without its blossom, it may be mistaken for just a tuft of grass.

However, when in bloom, this plant, a relative of the common flower-garden Daffodil, can brighten walks and hikes even on the dreariest of foggy or rainy days as its yellow blossoms line pathways in dry woods and dot the swaying vegetation of open meadows. In her book *The Concise Encyclopedia of Favorite Wild Flowers,* Marjorie J. Dietz says that Yellow Star Grass is "bound to be overlooked by those who value size and flamboyance first." Make sure you are not one of these heedless persons; stop to appreciate all the different parts of this delicate plant.

Its petals and sepals are impossible to tell apart, so botanists call them "tepals." Lifting the flower onto your fingers, you will notice the underside is hairy and has a greenish tint. Tiny hairs are also evident on the narrow leaves, which is why the plant was given the species name *hirsuta,* Latin for "hairy." The genus name *Hypoxis* is a combination of two Greek words meaning "pointed (or sharp) below," a reference to the shape of the plant's black seeds, which are a favorite food of bobwhites.

Some places you may encounter Yellow Star Grass include: Noland Divide Trail and Rich Mountain Road in GSMNP; BRP mileposts 55.1 and 218.7; and Homestead Trail at Mountain Lake Resort in Giles County, Virginia.

WILD OATS

Uvularia sessilifolia

Wild Oats is also known as Sessile Bellwort, "sessile" being a botanical term for a leaf that has no stalk but attaches directly to the stem. The "bell" part of the name is an obvious reference to the bell-shaped flowers. The word "wort" is from the Old English, but authorities disagree as to exactly what it means. Some say it comes from *wyrt,* which means either "herb" or "root," while others claim "wort" is simply another word for plant. Other sources say the word implies that a plant has some worth as a medication.

Liking partial shade, rich soil, and moist conditions, Wild Oats has a number of similar-looking relatives that may be seen in the Blue Ridge and Great Smoky Mountains. The stem of the Perfoliate Bellwort (*Uvularia perfoliata*) pierces the leaves that grow around its base, and the inside of the flower has rough, grainy, orange glands. Large-Flowered Bellwort (*Uvularia grandiflora*) grows up to twenty-four inches tall, has flowers up to two inches long, and has leaves whose undersides are covered in a whitish down. Mountain Bellwort (*Uvularia pudica*), found only from Virginia to Georgia, most closely resembles Wild Oats, but its leaves are a brighter green and the stem is slightly downy.

Other common names that have been applied to all the Bellworts include Merrybells, Cowbells, Strawbells, and Haybells.

Some places you may encounter one of the Bellworts include: Rich Mountain Road, and Ash Hopper, Noland Divide, Cades Cove Nature, and Kanati Fork Trails in GSMNP; BRP mileposts 44.4, 260.3, 272, 337.2, and 448.1; on the AT between Rocky Mountain and Moreland Gap in Georgia, Siler Bald in North Carolina, north slope of Pearis Mountain in southwest Virginia, and between Thunder Hill and Petites Gap in central Virginia; and north end of Big Savage Hiking Trail in Garrett County, Maryland.

FLOWER:
The yellow, elongated, bell-shaped flowers are about an inch long and droop (singly or in pairs) from the leaf axils.

LEAVES AND STEM:
The plant averages six to twelve inches in height, while the three-inch lance-shaped leaves, light green above and whitish below, have no stalks and are arranged oppositely.

BLOOM SEASON:
May to June

116

FLAME AZALEA
Rhododendron
calendulaceum

The pistils and stamens project far out from the five petals of the two-inch-wide yellow to orange to red, trumpet-shaped flowers.

The one- to four-inch-long leaves are hairy along the margins with scattered hairs above and stiff hairs along the midrib below. Unlike the evergreen leaves of some members of the Heath family, the Flame Azalea's leaves are deciduous.

May to June

The Flame Azalea's rich color makes its glorious flower stand out well against the rich undergrowth of the Blue Ridge and Great Smoky Mountains. William Bartram, the famous naturalist who explored the southern Appalachians during the 1700s, was so moved by the shrub that he wrote in his book *Travels* that the "fiery Azalea, flaming on the ascending hills or wavy surface of the gilding glades . . . that suddenly opening to view from dark shades, we are alarmed with the apprehension of the hill being set on fire. This is certainly the most gay and brilliant flowering shrub yet known."

Pink Azalea (*Rhododendron nudiflorum;* see page 154) is similar in appearance but with pink and fragrant flowers, while Early Azalea (*Rhododendron roseum*) is found on the Appalachian Trail between Humpback Mountain and Humpback Rocks in central Virginia. As the name implies, the white blossoms of Swamp Azalea (*Rhododendron viscosum*) are most often seen in moist environments.

You can recognize the Azaleas in winter by the different-sized buds that are bunched together at the end of the twigs. The larger ones, which are at the very tip of the twig, are the flower buds, while the smaller ones crowded just below are the branch and leaf buds.

Some places you may encounter Flame Azalea include: Chunky Gal Trail in Clay County, North Carolina; Andrews Bald and Heintooga Ridge Road in GSMNP; BRP mileposts 138.6, 144–145, 164–166, 217–221, 308–310, 368–380, and 412–423; on the AT on Blood Mountain in Georgia, and Muskrat Creek Shelter and Wayah Bald in North Carolina; and Bear Cliffs Trail at Mountain Lake Resort in Giles County, Pandapas Pond Trail in Montgomery County, Dragon's Tooth Trail in Craig County, and Whetstone Ridge Trail in Rockbridge County, Virginia.

BLUEBEAD LILY

Clintonia borealis

FLOWER:

Somewhat nodding, the inch-long flowers have three petals and three petal-like sepals that curve slightly backward and grow atop a six- to sixteen-inch stalk.

LEAVES AND STEM:

The basal, upright, oblong leaves are five to ten inches long.

BLOOM SEASON:

May to July

Favoring cool, moist woods with acidic soil, Bluebead Lily is most common in the evergreen forests of New England. However, it does range throughout the Appalachian Mountains and can be found in abundant colonies in the South—such as in the Spruce-Fir forests of the Great Smoky Mountains National Park or on the higher elevations of Virginia's Blue Ridge. This penchant for chilly environments is reflected in its species name, *borealis*. Like its relative Speckled Wood Lily (*Clintonia umbellulata;* see page 48), its genus name, *Clintonia,* honors De Witt Clinton, a governor of New York and a noted amateur naturalist of his day.

Native Americans used the plant to treat burns, infections, and problems of the heart, and to help reduce the pain of childbirth. Modern science has found that the rootstock of the plant contains an anti-inflammatory, proving how some treatments in folk medicine are accurate. Late in the summer, the flowers develop into the rich blue berries (beware, they are slightly poisonous) that give the plant its name. Other common names include Yellow Clintonia, Cow-Tongue, Clinton's Lily, Corn Lily, and Yellow Bead Lily.

Those who have studied the Lily family believe it includes 250 genera and close to 6,000 species worldwide. Among them are Turk's-Cap Lily (*Lilium superbum;* see page 138), the Solomon's Seals (*Polygonatum spp.;* see page 44), the False Solomon's Seals (*Smilacina spp.;* see page 50), and the Trilliums (*Trillium spp.;* see pages 30 and 252–253).

Some places you may encounter Bluebead Lily include: Joyce Kilmer Memorial Forest and Hangover Lead South Trail in the Joyce Kilmer–Slickrock Wilderness in North Carolina; Spruce-Fir Nature Trail and Clingmans Dome Road in GSMNP; BRP milepost 308.2; and on the AT on Apple Orchard Mountain in central Virginia, and Hawksbill Mountain in SNP.

WHORLED
LOOSESTRIFE

Lysimachia quadrifolia

Borne on threadlike stalks that emanate from the leaf axils, the small, star-shaped, yellow blossoms of the Whorled Loosestrife have a bit of red in their centers (which may radiate outward in thin lines). The one pistil extends beyond the five stamens.

The light green, lanceolate leaves grow in whorls of (usually) four along a stem that reaches heights of one to three feet.

Late May to August

Like bright, shining stars glowing amid darker celestial bodies, the yellow and red flowers of the Whorled Loosestrife stand out from the greenery of its foliage. This is not a plant that lets you go by it without noticing it.

In an open woodlands setting, it grows so tall that it rises above much of the undergrowth. Its whorls of leaves make it stand out from the other vegetation in clearings and fields, and its ability to grow in the sunshine makes it a common sight along winding country roads. In all cases, it is hard to miss the yellow flowers that, in the slightest of breezes, sway back and forth on their thin, wiry, green stalks.

As a rebuff to Great Britain and a rejection of the tea tax, colonists refused to drink commercial tea. Instead, they brewed what they called "Liberty Tea," made from the leaves of Loosestrifes. If your feet hurt, you should know that crushed Loosestrife leaves have been used to treat injuries inflicted by ill-fitting shoes.

Also found in the Blue Ridge and Great Smoky Mountains are Fringed Loosestrife (*Lysimachia ciliata*), whose leaves are slightly hairy and do not grow in whorls, and Lance-Leaved Loosestrife (*Lysimachia lanceolata*), whose narrower leaves also do not grow in whorls. Members of the genus *Lysimachia* are not true Loosestrifes but belong to the Primrose family. True Loosetrifes include the genus *Lythrum*, such as Spiked (or Purple) Loosestrife (*Lythrum salicaria*).

Some places you may encounter one of the Loosestrifes include: Hangover Lead South Trail in the Joyce Kilmer–Slickrock Wilderness in North Carolina; BRP mileposts 235, 242.3, 248.1, 252.8, 277.9, 289.6, 304.7, 364.5, and 458.2; and on the AT on Tray Mountain in Georgia, near Campbell Shelter spring, side trail to Sunset Field, and south of Punchbowl Shelter in central Virginia, and in Michaux State Forest in Pennsylvania.

PALE JEWELWEED

Impatiens pallida

Seek out Pale Jewelweed growing beside a stream or along a moist area in midsummer, and you will have a good chance of getting to watch one or more ruby-throated hummingbirds flit from flower to flower. The birds' long bills enable them to get deep inside the flower to obtain the nectar; in doing so, they pick up pollen from the stamens and deposit it onto the pistils of the next flower they visit.

Bees and other insects are usually too small to reach the nectar, but by nipping the back of the blossom—like they also do to the spurs of Columbine (*Aquilegia canadensis;* see page 168)—they can still get a taste of the sweet treat.

Also commonly found in the region is Spotted Jewelweed (*Impatiens capensis;* see page 252). Its flowers are a bit smaller and orangish-yellow with many spots, but the spur is longer.

Folk medicine has long held that the juice from the Jewelweed's succulent stem will help relieve the itch of poison ivy or stinging nettle. Other common names include Snapweed, Touch-Me-Not (in reference to its seedpods, which pop open when touched), Speckled Jewels, and Weather Cock. It has also been called Silverweed and Shining Grass because the bottom part of its leaf will become shiny (or silvery) after being exposed to water.

Some places you may encounter one of the Jewelweeds include: Falls Creek Falls Trail on Cherohala Skyway, and Slick Rock Creek Trail in the Joyce Kilmer–Slickrock Wilderness in North Carolina; Sugarlands Nature and Little River Trails in GSMNP; BRP mileposts 8.8, 78.4, 230.1, 290.5, 359.9, and 411; Lake Trail at Lake Robertson near Lexington, and Crabtree Falls Trail in Nelson County, Virginia; Mill Prong Trail in SNP; and south of Right Hand Fork Road on the Catoctin Trail in Frederick County, Maryland.

BUTTERFLY WEED

Asclepias tuberosa

Growing in bulbous terminal clusters of about two inches in length, each flower is less than a half inch in size and has five reflexed petals with a crown above.

The narrow leaves, which may be as much as six inches long, grow alternately on the one- to two-and-a-half-foot, hairy stem that branches near the top.

June to September

The long-blooming Butterfly Weed is easy to spot: rising fourteen to thirty inches high along woodland borders, roads, and clearings, its brilliant orange clusters wave in the breeze in the warmest months of the year. It received its species name, *tuberosa,* because what looks like a patch of several different plants above ground may really be branches, or clones, connected to each other by underground tubers.

Of course, its common name comes from its attractiveness to a variety of butterflies, such as fritillaries, swallowtails, hairstreaks, and coppers. Like other members of the Milkweed family, such as Common Milkweed (*Asclepias syriaca;* see page 182), it plays an important role in the life cycle and long migrations of the monarch butterflies.

Other names include Pleurisy Root, which derives from Native Americans' and early settlers' using the plant to treat lung problems, and Chigger Weed, which derives from the plant's growing in the same environment inhabited by the pesky mites.

Butterfly Weed has a seemingly haphazard, and almost sinister, way of managing pollination. Early each day, tiny drops of nectar form on the center of the individual flowers, inviting insects to stop by for a morning snack. Upon alighting, the visitor's leg may slip into a slit located on the crown, and a large pouch of pollen will attach itself. If the insect is strong enough to pull free with such a heavy load, it will visit another flower—where the pollen must be deposited in just the right spot on the crown for fertilization to occur. If the insect is too weak to fly away, it will die with its leg trapped in the slit.

Some places you may encounter Butterfly Weed include: Cades Cove and Abrams Creek Trail in GSMNP; BRP mileposts 63–65, 90, and 238–246; and Iron Mountain Trail in Smyth County, and along Breckinridge Mill Road (VA 600) in Botetourt County, Virginia.

COMMON MULLEIN

Verbascum thapsus

The fragrant yellow flowers grow in a dense cluster near the top of the stem. Each one-inch blossom has five lobes, five stamens, and one pistil.

The two- to seven-foot stem rises from a rosette of woolly, basal, one-inch leaves. The decurrent (meaning their stalks, or bases, extend along the outside of the stem) leaves get progressively smaller toward the top of the stem.

June to September

Through the centuries, humans have employed the Common Mullein, also known as Great Mullein and Wooly Mullein, in a variety of ways. In ancient Greece, the leaves were dried and used as wicks for candles and oil lamps; Roman armies soaked the tall, slender stems in oil and used them as torches. Generations of poor people have lined their shoes and stockings with the leaves to keep warm during cold weather, and early settlers used the absorbent leaves for diapers. In fact, if you find yourself having to answer the call of nature while on a woodland walk, you may be happy to know that America's pioneers considered the leaves to be some of the forest's best toilet paper.

The plant's mucilage, full of tannin, has been found to soothe hemorrhoids as well as other skin problems. A study has shown that it is also an effective anti-inflammatory. In addition, a tea made from Common Mullein leaves, which possess expectorant properties, can help soothe sore throats and relieve coughing and laryngitis. An oil obtained from the flowers has been prescribed for earaches.

Clasping-Leaved (or Orange) Mullein (*Verbascum phlomoides*) is similar to Common Mullein but has darker leaves that are not decurrent, larger flowers, and more branches. Moth Mullein (*Verbascum blattaria*) is a slenderer plant whose flowers are not as tightly bunched on the end of the stem.

Some places you may encounter one of the Mulleins include: low elevations in GSMNP; BRP mileposts 267.1, 294, 380, 399.7, and 411; roadsides in Sky Meadows State Park, open areas of Ivy Creek Natural Area in Albemarle County, and the Main Bikeway of Blackwater Creek Natural Area in Lynchburg, Virginia; and roadsides in Catoctin Mountain Park and beside the C&O Canal in Maryland.

EVENING PRIMROSE

Oenothera biennis

You know those time-lapse movies that show a flower opening up over the course of several hours or days? Well, position yourself next to a patch of Evening Primroses as the day draws to a close and you will get to experience the same thing, except this wonderful performance of nature's will not be on film but in the real world—and it will happen within minutes, not days.

Although some take longer than others, individual Evening Primrose blossoms have been observed fully opening within fifteen minutes. Don't despair if you miss the evening presentation, for a reverse of the process will happen within a few hours of sunlight shining upon the plant the next day.

Some Native Americans and early colonists ate the plants' seeds and first-year roots (the roots become too tough in subsequent years), while the Ojibwa Indians made a concoction from the plant to apply to wounds. The Shakers made a tea from the seeds to relieve indigestion.

Today, powders and oils made from the seeds can be found in natural and health food stores throughout the world. They are believed to be an effective treatment for a host of ailments including headaches, menstrual cramps, scabies, eczema, pain, and the dry mouth caused by Sjögren's syndrome.

Studies have shown that the seeds' oil is rich in an essential fatty acid known as gamma linolenic acid (GLA), and researchers believe it may be useful in preventing heart attacks and strokes, treating multiple sclerosis, and prolonging the life of those who are HIV-positive.

Some places you may encounter Evening Primrose include: along NC 276 between Brevard and Asheville, North Carolina; near the beginning of the Henry Lanum Trail in Nelson County, Virginia; and BRP mileposts 307.5, 308.2, 337.2, 432.7, and 457.9.

FLOWER:

The lemon-scented flowers, which are one to two inches across, have four notched petals, four reflexed sepals, eight yellow stamens, and noticeably X-shaped stigmas.

LEAVES AND STEM:

The hairy, sometimes purple-tinted stem often rises six to seven feet from the ground. The lanceolate leaves are alternate, hairy, and slightly toothed, and are two to seven inches long.

BLOOM SEASON:

June to September (or early October)

BLACK-EYED SUSAN

Rudbeckia hirta

FLOWER:

The flower of the Black-Eyed Susan is quite complex. The blossom grows at the end of a single stem, and its center cone is made up of hundreds of small florets that produce seeds and bloom in a ring around the cone. Connected to the cone and radiating outward are ten to twenty long, orange-yellow rays.

LEAVES AND STEM:

The two- to seven-inch leaves are lance-shaped (but may be a bit ovate), have distinct veins, and grow alternately on a stem of one to three feet in height. Both the leaves and the stem are slightly hairy.

BLOOM SEASON:

June to October

Lightly run your fingers up and down the stem of a Black-Eyed Susan and you will feel the small barbs that have evolved to keep unwanted insects and other creatures from crawling up and stealing the plant's abundant nectar and pollen. The plant does reward flying visitors who possess tongues long enough to reach inside the florets to sip the nectar, while those with short tongues may access the yellow pollen.

Early settlers used the plant as a diuretic, while some Native American tribes made a yellow dye from the flowers and a tea from the root to relieve cold symptoms. Modern herbalists state that the root extracts stimulate the immune system, and some doctors are now studying the plant to see if it may be useful in treating AIDS.

Although a native of the North American prairies that now populates much of the United States, Black-Eyed Susan is named for two Swedish botanists. By dubbing the genus *Rudbeckia*, Linnaeus, the father of the scientific system of names, honored a father and son, Olaus (or Olaf) Rudbeck Sr. and Jr., who had once tutored him. The common name "Black-Eyed" refers to the flower's center, which is actually more dark brown than black.

Some places you may encounter Black-Eyed Susan include: roadsides in Floyd County, Georgia; Indian Gap in GSMNP; BRP mileposts 38.8, 78.4, 162.4, 251, 277.9, 308.2, 339.5, 409.4, and 446; on the AT between Beech Gap and Big Spring Shelter in North Carolina, south of Street Gap along the North Carolina–Tennessee border, and numerous Skyline Drive crossings in SNP; and Andy Layne Trail in Botetourt County, Hawk Creek Trail at Lake Robertson near Lexington, and Freer Trail in Blackwater Creek Natural Area in Lynchburg, Virginia.

BUTTER-AND-EGGS

Linaria vulgaris

The irregular, one-inch-long, yellow flower (the "butter") is two-lipped. The upper lip is two-lobed, while the lower, three-lobed, spreading lip has a prominent blotch of orange (the "egg").

Butter-and-Eggs attains a height of one to three feet, with the approximately two-inch, grasslike leaves growing alternately on the upper part of the stem, and the lower leaves appearing opposite or in whorls.

June to October

Butter-and-Eggs is one of those wildflowers that has so many common names that it would be next to impossible to remember all of them. The plant was called Gallwort because farmers fed it to chickens in the belief that it would eliminate gallstones; they also named it Devil's Flower because, once it invaded a field or pasture, it was hard to eradicate. The name Ranstead or Ramstead refers to a person, known only as Mr. Ramstead, who was supposedly the first person to import the flower into North America. A thorough search to find the origin of the name Impudent Lawyer produced no results—which may just be appropriate.

Among the dozens of other names are Brideweed, Snapdragon, Yellowrod, Flaxseed, Peddler's Basket, Wild Tobacco, Rabbit's Weed, Continental Flower, and Jacob's Ladder.

Following the Doctrine of Signatures, the plant, with its resemblance to a mouth and throat, was used to treat sore gums and throat ailments. Those who were constipated made a tea from the flowers, while others used it to treat jaundice. The flowers were mixed into skin lotions, and the juices have been blended with milk for use as a pesticide.

Inhabitants of the British Isles appear to have ascribed mystical powers to the plant, as those who lived in England held that the seeds would ward off bad luck. The Scots believed you could break evil spells by walking several times around a patch of Butter-and-Eggs.

Some places you may encounter Butter-and-Eggs include: BRP mileposts 8.8, 10.9, and 26.3; and on the AT on Max Patch in North Carolina, and between Black Horse Gap and Bear Wallow Gap, and on Cold Mountain in central Virginia, and north of Doyle River Parking Area in SNP.

GOLDENROD

Solidago spp.

FLOWER:
Arranged in showy clusters along the upper branches, the individual flowers are small, not much more than one-eighth inch in size.

LEAVES AND STEM:
The leaves, which may be up to eight inches in length, are arranged alternately on stems that may be more than seven feet high.

BLOOM SEASON:
June to October

The Goldenrods are some of the last wildflowers to provide roadsides, fields, and meadows with a bit of color before the dull grays and browns of winter set in. Loaded with pollen, they attract scores of insects, including the bumblebee, praying mantis, and beetle. If you have a bit of the voyeur in you, hang around and watch the flower clusters for a while—visiting insects often use the plants as a romancing place. Of course, you may observe some violence in addition to the sex, as predators, such as spiders, lie in wait for the revelers to become oblivious to the dangers around them.

Goldenrod has been used to treat a large array of human ailments, and its genus name of *Solidago* reflects its capabilities, being translated from the Latin as "to heal" or "to make whole." Inflammation of the liver or urinary tract, kidney stones, arthritis, congestion, laryngitis, eczema, conjunctivitis, ulcers, yeast infections, gallstones, and more are said to respond favorably to various concoctions made from different parts of the plants.

Dozens of Goldenrod species grow in our area. Among them are Tall Goldenrod (*Solidago altissima;* see page 255), whose leaves are not noticeably toothed and its flowers larger than those of most of its relatives, while the blossoms of Skunk Goldenrod (*Solidago glomerata*) occur in looser terminal clusters that stand erect. In all of the world, it is only found in North Carolina and Tennessee.

Some places you may encounter one of the Goldenrods include: Cades Cove, Thunderhead, Balsam Mountain Road, and Clingmans Dome Trail in GSMNP; BRP mileposts 8.8, 78.4, 154.1, 230.1, 301.8, 355.3, 403.8, and 467.8; on the AT on Doll Flats in North Carolina, and between Reeds Gap and Rockfish Gap in central Virginia; and Hawk Creek Trail at Lake Robertson near Lexington, and Freer Trail in Blackwater Creek Natural Area in Lynchburg, Virginia.

137

TURK'S-CAP LILY

Lilium superbum

In a season in which the Daisies, Asters, and Goldenrods of the open meadows tend to predominate among the wildflowers, it is always a surprise and pleasure to come across the tall and showy Turk's-Cap Lily rising from the rich soil to bloom in the deep shade of a cove hardwood forest.

There are few recorded medicinal or alimentary uses for the plant, except that in *The Maine Woods* Henry David Thoreau wrote about the Native Americans of New England adding the plant's bulbs to soups.

Tiger Lily (*Lilium tigrinum*) is a native of eastern Asia but has escaped from gardens and established itself locally in the wild. Although its flowers are similar to those of the Turk's-Cap Lily, its leaves do not grow in whorls but are arranged alternately along the stem and have bulblets in their axils. Carolina Lily (*Lilium michauxii*) generally has only one to three flowers on a shorter stem. The blossoms are also smaller and usually lack the green "star." Orange-red Gray's Lily (*Lilium grayi;* see page 254) is found in only a few places in the region.

Members of the Lily family were some of the first flowers to be recorded in history, and paintings of them have been found in the palaces of ancient Greece, where the Lily was considered the flower of Hera, goddess of the moon. A legend within the Christian faith says that Lilies developed from the tears that Eve shed when she learned of her banishment from Eden.

Some places you may encounter Turk's-Cap Lily include: along Newfound Gap and Heintooga Ridge Roads in GSMNP; BRP mileposts 187.6, 294, 364–368, 406–411, 450.5, and 460.8; on the AT south of Gooch Gap and Henry Gap in Georgia, Cheoah Bald and north and south of Bly Gap in North Carolina, and Apple Orchard Mountain, Bald Knob, and The Priest in central Virginia; and Mount Rogers Trail in Smyth County, Virginia.

FLOWER:

The large (five-inch-wide), orange, nodding flowers have three petals and three sepals of the same size and color that curve sharply backward. A green line at the base of each forms a star where they meet. The projecting stamens are tipped with dangling anthers.

LEAVES AND STEM:

The lanceolate leaves grow in whorls up a stem three to seven feet tall.

BLOOM SEASON:

July to August

SMOOTH FALSE FOXGLOVE

Aureolaria laevigata

The one- to one-and-a-half-inch, trumpet-shaped flowers have five flaring lobes.

The one- to four-inch, lanceolate to elliptical leaves grow opposite along the one- to five-foot stem. The lower leaves are pinnately lobed, while the upper ones are less noticeably lobed, or unlobed.

July to September

Smooth False Foxglove, also known as Entire-Leaf False Foxglove, is slightly parasitic upon the roots of oak trees, which is why you may sometimes see it growing in dry, open forestlands alongside Squawroot (*Conopholis americana;* see page 108), another plant that parasitizes the oaks.

Found within the Blue Ridge and Great Smoky Mountains is another species that is also known as Smooth False Foxglove (*Aureolaria flava*). It has larger flowers and leaves that are more noticeably lobed. Fern-Leaved False Foxglove (*Aureolaria pedicularia*) is characterized by its many sticky and hairy branches with fernlike leaves. Other species that are similar in appearance to the ones already mentioned may be found in the region, although some may have purple flowers.

When looking to other sources for information on False Foxgloves, you should be aware that some reference books list them as being in the *Gerardia* genus. The name honors John Gerarde, who was the head gardener for Lord Brughley, minister of state for Queen Elizabeth around the turn of the seventeenth century. His *Herball* is recognized as one of the first botanical books to be published in English.

The False Foxgloves are named for their resemblance to the true Foxgloves, members of the genus *Digitalis.* A whimsical folk legend asserts that fairies gave the flowers to foxes to wear over their paws so that they would not be heard when raiding henhouses.

Some places you may encounter one of the False Foxgloves include: Tsali Trail in Graham County, and Yellow Mountain Trail in Jackson County in North Carolina; Cades Cove, Heintooga Ridge Road, and Laurel Falls and Sugarlands Nature Trails in GSMNP; and on the AT near Three Forks in Georgia, Iron Mountain and south of Buzzard Rock in southwest Virginia, and near Johns Hollow and Bryant Ridge Shelters in central Virginia.

Yellow-Fringed Orchid

Habenaria ciliaris

Growing in large terminal clusters, the flowers of the Yellow-Fringed Orchid have a lower lip that is deeply fringed and can be almost three-quarters of an inch in length. A one-and-a-half-inch, slim spur extends backward and downward from the base of the flower.

The leaves are lanceolate and sheath the stem, which may reach a height of two feet. The lower leaves can grow to be ten inches long, while the upper ones are much shorter.

July to September

Like the Turk's-Cap Lily (*Lilium superbum;* see page 138), the long-lasting blossoms of Yellow-Fringed Orchid appear in July. They are a welcome sight where their "creamsicle" color persists in a late-summer forest that is nearly a monotone green and almost devoid of any other conspicuously bright wildflowers. Besides open woodlands, the plant may be found on dry hillsides and in meadows, grassy bogs, and peaty soils.

The Cherokee Indians of the Blue Ridge and Great Smoky Mountains area made a hot tea from the roots to treat diarrhea, while a cold infusion was used to relieve headaches. In addition, they put a bit of the raw root on their fishhooks because experience seemed to show that it attracted more fish than using other bait by itself. The Seminoles used the root, both internally and externally, for snakebites. (There is no evidence that this was effective, so be sure to seek immediate medical help if you are bitten.)

When looking to other sources for information on Yellow-Fringed Orchid, you should be aware that some reference books place it within the genus *Platanthera*.

Seen much less often in the Blue Ridge and Great Smoky Mountains, the Orange-Fringed (also called Crested-Fringed) Orchid (*Habenaria cristata*) has smaller flowers with shorter lips and spurs, while the leaves are narrower, more pointed, and fewer in number. These two orchids sometimes cross-fertilize and hybridize, so it may be hard to tell exactly which species you have come across. As its name implies, Large Purple-Fringed Orchid (*Habenaria grandiflora;* see page 254) has purple blossoms.

Some places you may encounter Yellow-Fringed Orchid include: Steels Creek Trail in Burke County, North Carolina; along US 129 between Deels Gap and Chilhowee in Tennessee; Heintooga Ridge Road in GSMNP; and the AT between Tellico Gap and Wesser Bald in North Carolina.

GREEN-HEADED CONEFLOWER

Rudbeckia laciniata

Growing on long stalks, the two-to four-inch flower head has a rounded central disk of greenish-yellow flowers surrounded by bright yellow rays that may be more than an inch long.

The lower leaves have stalks and are often divided into deeply cut leaflets. The upper leaves are similar, but stalkless, and may be merely toothed and not deeply cut. The entire plant can reach a height of more than ten feet.

July to October

At a glance it is easy to mistake Green-Headed Coneflower for Black-Eyed Susan (*Rudbeckia hirta;* see page 132). However, look a little more closely and you will see that the Coneflower has a smooth stem (as opposed to one covered in bristles) and fewer rays emanating from its disk flowers, which are a greenish-yellow and not the dark brown of the Black-Eyed Susan. The rays are actually sterile flowers whose main purpose appears to be to serve as a landing pad and an attractant to the insects that will visit and pollinate the fertile disk flowers.

Naming the genus *Rudbeckia*—after Swedish botanists and father and son Olaus (or Olaf) Rudbeck Sr. and Jr.—Linnaeus said, "So long as the earth shall survive and as each spring shall see it covered with flowers, the Rudbeckia will preserve your glorious name."

Growing most often in the higher elevations of the Blue Ridge and Great Smoky Mountains, Green-Headed Coneflower can be found in a variety of environments, including in meadows and fields, moist woodlands, and thickets, and on stream banks and roadsides. Also known as Wild Golden-Glow, Cutleaf Coneflower, and Tall Coneflower, the plant has roots that Native Americans used to make a tea for indigestion. Young shoots were cooked and eaten in spring as a treat—and a change from the bland and "ungreen" diet of winter. Modern researchers have found that all members of the *Rudbeckia* genus contain immune-system stimulants that may hold promise in treating AIDS.

Some places you may encounter the Green-Headed Coneflower include: Balsam Mountain Campground, Clingmans Dome Trail and parking lot in GSMNP; and BRP mileposts 10.9, 36, 139, 161.2, 228.1, 304.7, 314, 359–368, 421.7, 427.5, 430.6, and 460.8.

HORSE BALM

Collinsonia canadensis

The fringes along the lower lip of the Yellow-Fringed Orchid (*Habenaria ciliaris;* see page 142) are so obvious that you can see them from several feet away, but those on the blossom of the Horse Balm are so minute that you may need a magnifying glass to make them out. Although it is a member of the Mint family, the plant's tiny flowers have a distinct lemony scent, and the fragrance of the leaves has been likened to that of citronella.

Like most Mints, a refreshing tea (hot or cold) may be made from the leaves. Native Americans and early settlers drank it to relieve sore throats and cold symptoms. As a liniment, it is said to soothe sore muscles: the name Horse Balm comes from farmhands' rubbing it on the joints and muscles of horses returning from a hard day's work in the fields. A root infusion was used as an astringent and diuretic.

Other common names include Stoneroot, for the root's resemblance to a stone, and Richweed, because the plant grows best in nutrient-rich soils found most often in moist woodlands. The genus name *Collinsonia* honors Peter Collinson, a naturalist who lived in London during the 1700s and planted in his garden many of the flowers sent to him from America by John Bartram.

Some places you may encounter Horse Balm include: Chattahoochee Nature Center in Roswell, Georgia; Tsali Trail in Graham County, North Carolina; Balsam Mountain Road and Bote Mountain Trail in GSMNP; and BRP mileposts 294, 306.6, and 308.2.

FLOWER:

The yellow flowers, which are no more than a half inch wide, grow in loose clusters and are two-lipped, with the lower lip being longer and fringed. The stamens and pistil are noticeably longer than the rest of the blossom.

LEAVES AND STEM:

The egg-shaped leaves are sharply toothed, opposite, and as much as ten inches long but get smaller as they progress up the two- to four-foot stem.

BLOOM SEASON:

Late July to October

146

FILMY ANGELICA

Angelica triquinata

The individual flowers are minute, greenish-yellow to white, and grow in large umbels.

The large leaves are divided into three leaflets that may in turn be divided into three or five parts. As they progress up the two- to six-foot, purple-tinged stem, they become smaller.

August to September

The large umbel and, indeed, the entire look of Filmy Angelica is somewhat reminiscent of that of several of its relatives, such as Cow Parsnip (*Heracleum lanatum;* see page 70) and Queen Anne's Lace (*Daucus carota;* see page 62).

Some reference books place Filmy Angelica in with green flowers, others in the section that contains those with white petals; still others classify it as having yellow blossoms. All are correct, as any of these colors, or variations and combinations of them, may be present depending on its location or stage of blooming.

According to Dr. C. Ritchie Bell, founder of the North Carolina Botanical Gardens at the University of North Carolina–Chapel Hill, the plant produces prodigious amounts of nectar that is evidently intoxicating to the bees that feast upon it.

Purple Angelica (*Angelica atropurpurea*) is less common, has larger umbels, and is most often found in wet areas. Hairy Angelica (*Angelica venenosa*) has white flowers and is slightly hairy.

The Angelicas contain compounds similar to those found in the calcium channel blockers that are used to control blood pressure and angina, as well as other substances that help correct arrhythmia. The fresh roots are poisonous, but drying them eliminates the problem, and to save money, some perfume companies add Angelica root oil to the bottles of musk that they sell because the fragrances are similar.

Some places you may encounter Filmy Angelica include: The Boulevard Trail, and Clingmans Dome and Balsam Mountain Roads in GSMNP; Art Loeb Trail in Transylvania County, North Carolina; BRP mileposts 294.7, 339.5, 355, 359.9, 419.3, and 364.1–376.6; and on the AT on Roan Mountain, Round Bald, and Grassy Ridge along the North Carolina–Tennessee border.

SHARP-LOBED HEPATICA

Hepatica acutiloba

FLOWER:
Lacking petals, the nearly one-inch flowers have five to nine sepals that range from white to pink to lilac. Numerous stamens have pale anthers, while a small cluster of pistils is located at the center of the flower. Just below the flower are three green leaf bracts.

LEAVES AND STEM:
The two-inch-wide, three-lobed leaves grow from the base of the hairy stems.

BLOOM SEASON:
Late February to May

As they do for a number of flowers that bloom in late winter, ants help disseminate the Sharp-Lobed Hepatica's seeds. Attracted to oils and possibly other nutrients found in the bulges—known as elaiosomes—on the plant's seed casing, the ants bring the casings back to their tunnels and eat the elaiosomes. Because the rest of the casing is too hard to open, the ants discard the seed—which is then able to germinate and sprout within the safety of the tunnel.

Round-Lobed Hepatica (*Hepatica americana;* see page 255) has a similar appearance, but its leaf bracts and lobes are more rounded. Some botanists claim that the Sharp-Lobed is just a race, or subspecies, of the Round-Lobed Hepatica, and now refer to both as *Hepatica nobilis.* However, other authorities (somewhat grudgingly it would seem) accede to the one-species classification but say there are two subspecies—the round-lobed, known as *Hepatica nobilis obtuse,* and the sharp-lobed, designated *Hepatica nobilis acuta.* (Don't feel bad if you are confused; it appears everyone else is, too. It seems like we would have been better off if we had just kept the old names, doesn't it?) To add to this confusion, some reference books place the Hepaticas in the genus *Anemone.*

Because the three-lobed leaves remain on the stem throughout the winter to turn a liverish color, Hepatica has also been called Liverwort, Liver-moss, and Liverleaf.

Some places you may encounter one of the Hepaticas include: The Pocket on Pigeon Mountain in Walker County, Georgia; Joyce Kilmer Memorial Forest in North Carolina; Cove Hardwood Nature Trail and Tremont Road in GSMNP; BRP milepost 469.8; on the AT on Fork Mountain in central Virginia, and below Fishers Gap Overlook in SNP; in Ivy Creek Natural Area near Charlottesville, Virginia; and in the higher elevations of Catoctin Mountain Park in Maryland.

SPRING BEAUTY

Claytonia virginica

FLOWER:
The half-inch, white to pink flower has distinctive deeper pink veins coursing through its five petals.

LEAVES AND STEM:
Two leaves grow opposite each other about halfway up a four- to twelve-inch stem.

BLOOM SEASON:
March to May

To protect itself from chilly winds and temperatures, the Spring Beauty only opens its blossom when the sun is shining brightly, which is also when bees and other insects fly from bloom to bloom, helping pollinate the flowers.

A relative, the Carolina Spring Beauty (*Claytonia caroliniana*), has a very similar appearance, but its leaves are wider and its habitat is usually a slightly drier environment. The genus is named for John Clayton, who lived in Virginia during the eighteenth century and spent much of his time gathering wildflower specimens.

Black bears and, unfortunately, wild boars eat the Spring Beauty tubers. Imported from Europe near the turn of the twentieth century, a number of the hogs escaped, and their descendants now inhabit the Blue Ridge and Great Smoky Mountains.

Bears dig up the ground in search of food, but wild boars leave large patches of earth looking as if they had been churned over by a rototiller. The animals' rooting reduces the number of wildflowers, destroys the eggs and shelters of ground-nesting birds, and, because the boars are foreign to the mountains' ecosystem, are threatening native species. It is estimated that hundreds of wild boars inhabit Great Smoky Mountains National Park. In an effort to reduce the damage, the boars are trapped and moved to private hunting preserves. However, because they are such prolific breeders, trapping seems not to reduce their numbers but only keep them in check.

Some places you may encounter one of the Spring Beauties include: Clingmans Dome Road in GSMNP; BRP mileposts 359.9, 427.5, and 430.6; and on the AT between Unicoi Gap and Dicks Creek Gap in Georgia, Big Bald along the North Carolina–Tennessee border, and Pearis and Peters Mountains in central Virginia.

PINK AZALEA

Rhododendron nudiflorum

If you happen to walk by a couple of shrubs full of the Pink Azalea's fragrant blooms, the scent can be so strong that you might feel as if you have been spritzed by an employee of the perfume section of a department store. The habit of blossoming before the leaves appear gives the plant its species name, *nudiflorum,* basically translating as "coming into flower while still naked."

Although a member of the Heath family, the Pink Azalea has also been called Wild Honeysuckle and Purple Honeysuckle because the flower so resembles the Honeysuckle blossom. It is also commonly called Pinxter-Flower, although the reason for the name is in dispute: some people say it is simply a spelling variation of pink, while others maintain that it is derived, in a roundabout way, from the Greek word for the Pentecost, the seventh Sunday after Easter. While Azaleas in some parts of the world may bloom that late, the Pink Azaleas of the Blue Ridge and Smokies will be long gone.

When looking to other sources for information on the Pink Azalea, you should be aware that some reference books list it as *Rhododendron periclymenoides.*

Some places you may encounter Pink Azalea include: Foothills Parkway and Abrams Creek in GSMNP; BRP mileposts 4, 92–97, 138.6, 145.4, 154.5, 162.9, 211.6, 217–222, 350–351, and 412–423; on the AT on Pearis Mountain in southwest Virginia, and Bear Wallow Gap and between Humpback Mountain and Humpback Rocks in central Virginia; Signal Knob Trail in Shenandoah County, and Bald Mountain Trail in Augusta County, Virginia; and Big Savage Hiking Trail in Garrett County, and in higher elevations of Catoctin Mountain Park in Maryland.

REDBUD

Cercis canadensis

FLOWER:
The dark pink to deep purple flowers have five unequal petals, are about a half inch in size, and grow in clusters of four to eight on thin stalks.

LEAVES AND STEM:
The heart-shaped leaves are smooth along the edges, long-stalked, and have five to nine main veins. The Redbud has a short trunk, spreading branches, and most often grows no more than twelve to fifteen feet tall but may attain a height of forty feet.

BLOOM SEASON:
April to May

One of the showiest trees, the Redbud is a member of the Pea family. Long before its leaves appear, its branches and twigs become festooned with thick accumulations of dark pink to purple blossoms. In days past, the flowers were eaten in salads or fried and mixed with a meat dish.

The flowers, which do not begin to appear on the tree until it is four or five years old, are bisexual (meaning that they have both male and female parts) and are pollinated by insects. Once fertilized, they develop into two- to three-inch-long pods that are pointed at both ends and contain a row of flat beanlike seeds. If you are observant, you may be able to identify the tree when it is without flowers or leaves, as the pods often hang on well into winter.

The seeds are eaten by a few songbirds, such as bobwhites, and the roots have been used to produce a red dye.

Redbud is also known as the Judas Tree or Flowering Judas. According to a Christian legend, Judas Iscariot, having betrayed Jesus, hanged himself on a Eurasian species of Redbud that had white flowers. Ever since, the tree has blossomed red to show the shame of Judas and the blood he caused to be shed.

Some places you may encounter Redbud include: Pigeon Mountain in Walker County, Georgia; Little River Gorge in GSMNP; BRP mileposts 54–68; Stuart's Knob in Fairy Stone State Park, North Mountain Trail in Craig County, on the hillsides of Lake Robertson near Lexington, and Blackwater Creek Natural Area in Lynchburg, Virginia; and Green Ridge Hiking Trail in Allegany County, Maryland.

WILD GERANIUM

Geranium maculatum

The ingenuities of nature are seemingly infinite. Take a close look at the petals of a Wild Geranium flower and you will see dark blue lines leading from the outer edge to the center of the blossom. If you were a bee, these lines would be even more pronounced due to your ability to see ultraviolet light, and would direct you to land on the plant's reproductive parts, to deposit the pollen you picked up from the previous plant you visited, and thus insure the propagation of the species. (Incidentally, while the pollen of most plants is an orangish-yellow, that of the Wild Geranium is a brilliant blue. Researchers are not sure if this is also a mechanism to attract bees.)

After the petals drop off, an elongated ovary becomes part of the seedpod. As the seeds enlarge, they cause the pod to curl and become ever tighter. Eventually the pressure becomes too much and the pod bursts, catapulting the seeds as much as thirty feet. Another of nature's marvels now occurs: The seed has an appendage—botanists have dubbed it an awn—that, by shriveling when dry and expanding when wet, actually moves the seed along the ground until it drops into a crack or hole. The awn then pushes it further into the soil, where it has a safe place in which to germinate.

Some places you may encounter Wild Geranium include: Sugarlands Nature, Bud Ogle Nature, and Porters Creek Trails, and Newfound Gap Road in GSMNP; BRP mileposts 8.8, 84–86, 133.6, 170–172, 211.6, and 375; on the AT north of Winding Stair Gap in North Carolina, north of Angel's Rest in southwest Virginia, and Petites Gap, Reeds Gap, The Priest, and Humpback Mountain in central Virginia; Pandapas Pond Trail in Montgomery County, and woodlands of Sky Meadows State Park in Virginia; and roadsides in Catoctin Mountain Park in Maryland.

WILD BLEEDING HEART

Dicentra eximia

Resembling jewel pendants strung on a necklace, the Wild Bleeding Heart blossoms are arranged along the leafless stems according to age. The most mature flower, which may be ready to drop its petals, is closest to the main stem, while the smaller, possibly unopened blossoms, grow at the tip, where new buds are constantly forming during the blooming season.

The exotic shape of the flower, similar in appearance to its relative Squirrel Corn (*Dicentra canadensis;* see page 22), is pleasing to the human eye, but that, of course, is not its purpose. The outer petals that make up the "heart" are actually containers for the nectar. Two inner petals seal off the mouth of the containers and, forming the "drop of blood," extend downward. In search of the nectar, a visiting bee pushes against these inner petals, and a hinge at their base opens up, thrusting pollen onto the insect's body and allowing it access to the delectable liquid.

Other common names for Wild Bleeding Heart include Fringed Bleeding Heart, Plumy Bleeding Heart, and Turkey Corn. It came to be called "Staggerweed" when farmers discovered that their cattle would stumble and fall dead after grazing on the poisonous roots and leaves. Hold the flower upside down and pull the petals slightly apart and you will see how it came to be called Lady-in-the-Bath.

Some places you may encounter Wild Bleeding Heart include: Chattahoochee Nature Center in Roswell, Georgia; Little River Road, and Cosby Nature and Roaring Fork Motor Nature Trails in GSMNP; on the AT near Laurel Falls in Tennessee, Iron Mountain in southwest Virginia, and near Johns Hollow Shelter and south of Jennings Creek in central Virginia; and Crabtree Falls Trail in Nelson County, Virginia.

FLOWER:
The drooping flowers grow along a leafless stem that extends out from the rest of the plant. The two deeply rounded, outer petals form a "heart," while the two inner petals form the "drop of blood" that drips from the heart.

LEAVES AND STEM:
The ten-inch leaves are all basal, greatly divided, and persist long into the growing season. The entire plant may grow up to two feet tall.

BLOOM SEASON:
April to June

ROSY
TWISTED STALK

Streptopus roseus

FLOWER:
The open, bell-shaped flowers are less than a half inch long and have six pointed sepals that curve back as the blossom ages.

LEAVES AND STEM:
The two- to six-inch lanceolate leaves have deep parallel veins and fine hairs along the margins; they grow alternately on the one- to two-foot stem.

BLOOM SEASON:
April to June

Because it has similar-looking leaves, Rosy Twisted Stalk is sometimes mistaken for Smooth Solomon's Seal (*Polygonatum biflorum;* see page 44) or False Solomon's Seal (*Smilacina racemosa;* see page 50). However, neither have the zigzagging stem of the Rosy Twisted Stalk. The plant did not receive its common name from the way its main stem grows but rather for its flower, whose stalk twists around the stem from where it rises to the side of the leaf axil to have the flower end up dangling below the foliage. Later in the year, the flower develops into a rich red berry.

Favoring moist woodlands that remain cool throughout the year, the plant is near its natural southern limit when you find it in the spruce-fir forests in the higher elevations of the Great Smoky Mountains National Park.

When looking to other sources for information on Rosy Twisted Stalk, you should be aware that some reference books list it as *Streptopus lanceolatus.*

Rosy Twisted Stalk is also known as Rose Mandarin, Rose Twisted Stalk, and Sessile-Leaf Twisted Stalk. The latter name refers to the fact that the leaves have no stalk but attach directly to the stem. Also found in the Blue Ridge and Great Smoky Mountains, the larger Clasping-Leaf Twisted Stalk (*Streptopus amplexifolius*), also known as White Mandarin, has leaves that clasp the stem, and flowers that are usually greenish-white.

Some places you may encounter Rosy Twisted Stalk include: Deep Creek Trail in the Joyce Kilmer–Slickrock Wilderness, and Green Ridge Trail in Madison County, North Carolina; The Boulevard Trail and Newfound Gap Road in GSMNP; on the AT north of Newfound Gap in GSMNP; and Lostland Run Trail in Garrett County, Maryland.

SHOWY ORCHIS

Orchis spectabilis

FLOWER:
Emanating from the axils of the leaf bracts, there are several of the Showy Orchis blossoms arranged along a flower spike four to twelve inches tall. Each flower is about an inch long, has three sepals and two lateral petals that form a purple to pink hood, and a lower white lip that has a spur hanging from it.

LEAVES AND STEM:
Enveloping the bottom of the flower stalk are the two (sometimes three) widely ovate basal leaves. Each smooth leaf is four to eight inches long.

BLOOM SEASON:
April to June

One look at the Showy Orchis's flamboyant flower is all it takes to understand why it received the species name *spectabilis,* Latin for "spectacular."

Like other members of the Orchid family, it must have certain fungi present in the soil in order to survive. The seeds' outer shells are eaten by the fungi, while the seeds' inner parts obtain needed nourishment from the fungi. This relationship continues as the seed develops into a corm, the bulblike underground part of a flower stem where food is stored. The fungi delivers minerals and nutrients to the corm, which in turn provides the fungi with substances that the growing plant has produced through photosynthesis.

When looking to other sources for information on Showy Orchis, you should be aware that some reference books list it as *Galearis spectabilis.*

It was debated long and hard about whether or not to include specific sites where you may encounter Showy Orchis. Like all of the region's Orchids, it is having a hard time surviving the modern world and those who would unscrupulously dig it up. Please do not betray our trust in you—do not dig, pick, or disturb any Showy Orchis plant.

Some places you may encounter Showy Orchis include: Sosebee Cove in Union County, Georgia; Joyce Kilmer Memorial Forest in North Carolina; Lower Mount Cammerer Trail, and Bud Ogle, Roaring Fork Motor, and Cosby Nature Trails in GSMNP; BRP milepost 339.5; on the AT between High Rocks and Spivey Gap in North Carolina, and Thunder Ridge and between Long Mountain Wayside and Pedlar Lake in central Virginia; and Old Rag Fire Road in SNP.

FIRE PINK

Silene virginica

The pink in Fire Pink's name does not refer to the color of the flower but rather to the notch at the end of each petal that looks like the notches pinking shears make on fabric. The plant is also commonly called Catchfly for the sticky substance and tiny hairs along its stem that capture insects. Unlike the secretions of carnivorous (now often referred to as insectivorous) plants that are used to attract insects for consumption, the sticky substance on the Fire Pink is used only to prevent unwanted insects from reaching the nectar.

The genus name *Silene* also refers to this substance. Some authorities say the word is derived from Silenus, the foster father of Bacchus in Greek mythology. Silenus was said to be fond of drink and was often found passed out, his face covered in beer froth. Evidently some observers were reminded of this foam when they looked at the sticky secretions found on several members of the genus. Other people claim the genus name is simply a derivation of the Greek word for saliva, *sialon*.

Some places you may encounter Fire Pink include: Chunky Gal Trail in Clay County, North Carolina; Little River Road and Chestnut Top Trail in GSMNP; BRP mileposts 1–2, 85.8, 154.5, 241, 339.3, 367–375, and 404–408; on the AT between Springer Mountain and Stover Creek in Georgia, between Betty Creek Gap and Bear Pen Trail in North Carolina, and north of Dragon's Tooth in central Virginia; and Molly's Knob Trail in Hungry Mother State Park, Ribble Trail in Giles County, and Chessie Nature Trail in Rockbridge County, Virginia.

COLUMBINE

Aquilegia canadensis

FLOWER:
   The Columbine's flower is a nod-ding red and yellow blossom one to two inches long, with five petals curving upward as hollow spurs.

LEAVES AND STEM:
   The leaves are compound and divided into three; they grow on a one- to two-foot-tall stem.

BLOOM SEASON:
   April to July

When the sun shines on Columbine flowers at just the right angle, they can take on the appearance of interestingly shaped Japanese lanterns. Swaying to soft mountain breezes, the fine texture of the blossoms seems to soak up the light, causing them to become almost luminescent and to appear as if they are constructed of the finest rice paper saturated with rich, hand-painted watercolors.

The flower is designed to prevent self-pollination. The male parts—the stamens and anthers—mature first, starting from the outside ring and moving inward. By the time the female counterparts have developed, with the style pushing the feathery stigmas to emerge at the mouth of the flower, the anthers will have already shed their pollen. Some observers say that individual plants "exhaust" themselves by producing this abundance of flowers and pollen and so die within a few years. However, they produce so many seeds that other plants soon rise to take their place.

Native Americans mixed the seeds with tobacco to smoke during council meetings, as it was believed that the aroma facilitated amiable feelings. In the same vein, young men used the ground seeds as a love potion, rubbing them on their hands before caressing their mates.

Other common names include Culverwort, Meeting Houses, Jack-in-Trousers, and Rock Bells. The latter refers to the environment in which the flowers most often grow.

Some places you may encounter Columbine include: Chunky Gal Trail in Clay County, North Carolina; Thomas Divide Trail, and Heintooga Ridge and Laurel Creek Roads in GSMNP; BRP mileposts 74–75, 339.3, and 370–378; on the AT north of VA 624, and Petites Gap in central Virginia; Sky Meadows State Park, and Chessie Nature Trail in Rockbridge County, Virginia; and in the higher elevations of Catoctin Mountain Park, and Big Savage Hiking Trail in Garrett County, Maryland.

TRUMPET HONEYSUCKLE

Lonicera sempervirens

The Trumpet Honeysuckle is a hard flower to miss: its whorl of long floral tubes, bright red on the outside and yellow on the inside, loudly proclaim their presence against the background of the vine's rich green leaves. Like Spotted Jewelweed (*Impatiens capensis;* see page 252) and Trumpet Vine (*Campsis radicans;* see page 194), the flower has a deep throat and red color that make it attractive to ruby-throated hummingbirds, who are its main pollinators.

Linnaeus gave it the genus name *Lonicera* to honor Adam Lonicer (some references say Lonitzer), a sixteenth-century physician who published a book on natural history. The species name is from the Latin *semper,* for "ever" or "always," and *virens,* meaning "green," and refers to the plant's evergreen leaves. (However, the leaves do not stay green in the more northern parts of the United States.)

Trumpet Honeysuckle is a climbing vine that, while sometimes present in open forestlands, is most often found along woodland borders and thickets and growing upon fences and stone walls. Unlike the invasive Japanese Honeysuckle (*Lonicera japonica*), it is native to the area and not a pest plant. Other common names include Woodbine, Coral Honeysuckle, and the very descriptive Firecracker Vine.

Interestingly, the final upper leaves of the stalk (found just below the whorl of flowers) join together to appear to encircle the stem. This trait is shared with Glaucus Honeysuckle (*Lonicera dioica*), which has greenish-yellow flowers, and Yellow Honeysuckle (*Lonicera flava*), which has clusters of bright yellow flowers. All are found in the Blue Ridge and Great Smoky Mountains.

Some places you may encounter Trumpet Honeysuckle include: Cherokee Orchard Road in GSMNP, and along Skyline Drive, especially at milepost 57.3 in SNP.

170

GAYWINGS

Polygala paucifolia

Fringed Polygala. Fringed Milkwort. Flowering Wintergreen. Bird-on-the-Wing. Gaywings. No matter what common name is applied to these wonderfully shaped flowers, it is always a pleasure to find a colony of them, their purplish-pink blossoms causing them to stand out against the brown forest litter in which they grow. The plant is a Milkwort, whose family members are characterized by corolla tubes formed by three united petals, with the lower one being fringed, and a pair of wing-shaped sepals of a similar color.

Gaywings are usually found in small colonies rather than individually because they grow from creeping underground rootstocks as well as by seeds. Like Common Wood Sorrel (*Oxalis montana;* see page 52), Gaywings produce what are known as cleistogamous flowers. You will probably have to crouch to inspect the base of the plant to find them. Growing from small branchlets (that are often hidden underground), the cleistogamous flowers never really open, but instead self-fertilize, thereby insuring the propagation of the plant—if for some reason it fails to become fertilized by the pollen of another.

The federal government has listed Gaywings as endangered in several states, including Indiana, Ohio, and Kentucky.

Some places you may encounter Gaywings include: Tallulah Falls State Park in Georgia; Abrams Falls Trail in GSMNP; on the AT between Bluff Mountain and Hot Springs, between High Rocks and Spivey Gap in North Carolina, and north and south of VA 624, close to Jennings Creek, on Fork Mountain, and in James River Face Wilderness in central Virginia; Dragon's Tooth Trail in Craig County, Virginia; and along the Rocky Mount Trail in SNP.

MOUNTAIN LAUREL

Kalmia latifolia

FLOWER:
Growing in clusters, the nearly one-inch, cup-shaped flowers vary from pink to white. Radiating from the center, the flower's ten stamens create a distinctive spoke design.

LEAVES AND STEM:
The shrub usually grows from five to ten feet tall but can, on rare occasions, reach thirty-five feet.

BLOOM SEASON:
May to July

The evergreen leaves of the Mountain Laurel sometimes cause the plant to be confused with Great Rhododendron (*Rhododendron maximum;* see page 64), Carolina Rhododendron (*Rhododendron minus*), or Catawba Rhododendron (*Rhododendron catawbiensis;* see page 253). All these are members of the Heath family, but the Mountain Laurel's leaves are smaller and slenderer. Early settlers had a saying that helped them distinguish between the Rhododendrons and the Laurel: "Short leaf, short name; long leaf, long name."

Like those of the other Heaths, Mountain Laurel leaves contain a poison, andromedotoxin. Deer can eat the leaves without ill effect (as they also eat those of the poison ivy), but stories abound about animals who eat the deer and become gravely sick or die. (It is this poison that causes the leaves to snap and crackle when they burn.) Native Americans made a tea from the leaves that was used to commit suicide.

The genus name *Kalmia* honors Pehr Kalm, a Swede who roamed the eastern portion of North America in the mid-1700s collecting unknown species. A pupil of the famous botanist Linnaeus, Kalm returned to Europe with more than 600 specimens. His name for the Mountain Laurel was Spoon Tree because, as he reported in his journal, "The Indians used to make their spoons and trowels of its wood." The early colonists found another use for the hard wood by fashioning it into weavers' shuttles and pulley axles.

Some places you may encounter Mountain Laurel include: BRP mileposts 130.5, 162.9, 347.9, 380, and 400; on the AT on Blood Mountain, Laurel Fork Gorge in Tennessee, and in Michaux State Forest in Pennsylvania; Passamaquoddy Trail, and Old Rag in SNP; and trails of Rocky Gap State Park in Allegany County, Maryland.

INDIAN PAINTBRUSH

Castilleja coccinea

Reflecting the rich red sunsets for which the Blue Ridge and Great Smoky Mountains are known, Indian Paintbrush inhabits open meadows, sandy soils, thickets, and woodland borders and grows on roadsides. It is sunsets, in fact, that gave rise to the common name. An Indian brave trying to paint a picture of the evening sky became disconcerted because his collection of dyes could not do justice to the atmospheric display he was witnessing. In answer to his prayers, the Great Spirit sent him paintbrushes wet with vibrant hues. When finished painting, the brave tossed the brushes aside, and wherever one landed an Indian Paintbrush plant began to grow.

One source says that Native Americans made a love charm potion from the plant that was secretly added to food, yet another reference states that the plant was used as a poison to destroy enemies—guess it depends on your perception of who was a lover and who was an enemy!

By rights, this plant should probably have been placed with the green flowers but has instead been placed here because the deep scarlet leaf bracts are its most distinguishing feature.

Also known as Scarlet Paint-Cup, Indian Paintbrush belongs to a genus with more than 200 species, many of which may be found in the prairies and meadows of the western United States. *Castilleja lineariaefolia* is the state flower of Wyoming, where children chew on the juicy stems to form a tasty chewing gum. The genus is named for Domingo Castillejo, a famous Spanish botanist.

Some places you may encounter Indian Paintbrush include: along US 64 between Highlands and Brevard, and on the grounds of Linville Caverns on US 221 north of Ashford, North Carolina; Heintooga Ridge Road in GSMNP; BRP mileposts 369–371; and on the AT east of Woody Gap in Georgia.

GOAT'S RUE

Tephrosia virginiana

Here is a plant so common throughout the Blue Ridge and Great Smoky Mountains—in open fields and meadows, in dry woodlands, on roadsides, in thickets, and in sandy soils lacking nutrients—that it is often ignored. Yet, Goat's Rue has a beauty unmatched by many of the region's other flowers. The upper, yellowish-white petal, with distinct veins running its length, curls over to provide a protective hood for the lovely pink to purple flaring wings bracketing the inner keel, made up of two petals fused together.

The common name was coined by farmers who gave it to their goats because it grew abundantly and wild, making it a free source of feed. That practice has been discontinued because it is now known that the plant contains retenone, a poison used in commercially produced insecticides.

Other common names include Wild Sweet Pea, Dolly Varden, Cat Gut, and Devil's Shoestrings. The latter two refer to the plant's long, stringy roots, which are so strong that they made it hard for a farmer to till a field and reminded people of the material once used to string tennis rackets. Cherokee Indian women washed their hair in a tea made from the roots in the conviction that the strength of the plant's underground parts would transfer to their hair to keep it from splitting or falling out. Also believing that they could obtain strength from it, early American baseball players rubbed the tea on their arms, legs, and hands.

Some places you may encounter Goat's Rue include: Yellow Creek Mountain Trail in Graham County, North Carolina; along many roads in GSMNP; BRP milepost 304.6; and on the AT in Black Horse Gap and south of Highcock Knob in central Virginia.

SUNDEW

Drosera rotundifolia

"Feed me, Seymour, I'm hungry!" It is almost impossible to look at the Sundew and not think about the macabre plot from *The Little Shop of Horrors,* the B-grade science fiction movie that became a hit Broadway musical.

Surely the writers of this satirical, yet sinister, story were inspired in part by the way this insectivorous plant nourishes itself by attracting, capturing, and consuming unsuspecting victims. Glandular hairs on the small leaves are coated with a sweet, sticky fluid to attract insects, which become entangled in some of the longer outer hairs. The hairs grow in a spurt, adding cells that enable them to "fold" over the insect and draw it into more intimate contact with the leaf, where shorter hairs secrete digestive enzymes.

Early settlers rubbed the plant on their feet to make use of its proteolytic properties to eliminate bunions, corns, and warts. Modern research shows the plant contains carboxy-oxy-napthoquinone, a compound that, like codeine, calms cough-triggering muscle spasms. Another substance, plumbagin, has been found to fight off the bacteria that cause laryngitis and pneumonia.

The genus name *Drosera* is derived from the Greek word that means "wet" or "dewy," and refers to the sticky fluid secreted by the hairs. The species name, *rotundifolia,* translates from the Latin as "round leaves."

The environment in which Sundews are most often found—sphagnum bogs—is not all that common in the southern mountains of the eastern United States, which means that the plants are just as uncommon. Unfortunately, many people are fascinated by their insectivorous ways and see nothing wrong with harvesting them. For this reason, it was decided not to include in this book specific sites where you may encounter Sundew in the Blue Ridge and Great Smoky Mountains.

COMMON
MILKWEED

Asclepias syriaca

Milkweed is such a common plant that it is easy to overlook the vital role it plays in the web of life. However, monarch butterflies, those resolute little creatures that weigh less than an ounce and yet migrate thousands of miles every year, don't overlook it—their survival depends upon it. Leaving their winter home among the evergreens of the high-altitude forests in central Mexico, they head northward in late winter. Flying through Texas, they spread out into the southern portions of the United States—and this is where the Milkweed comes in. As they travel, they mate, but they will lay eggs only on the various species of Milkweed found in the United States and Canada. After laying eggs, the butterflies die and are replaced by a new generation that will travel further north before laying its eggs. Hopscotching from Milkweed to Milkweed, it will be the fourth or fifth generation that finally arrives in southern Canada.

Prompted by cooler temperatures and decreasing daylight, the monarchs begin the return journey in late summer. But they are genetically different from their ancestors. These southbound insects don't breed or lay eggs. Their lives consist of consuming nectar to fuel their flight to Mexico, where they spend the winter before the process repeats itself.

Common Milkweed is the plant whose seedpods you used to love to break open as a child so that you could watch hundreds of the tiny, feathery parachutes be whirled away by late-summer breezes.

Some places you may encounter Common Milkweed include: BRP mileposts 17.6, 85–86, 167–176, 243.4, 301.8, 403.8, and 444.5; Forest Service Road 845 in Smyth County, and Huckleberry Ridge Loop Trail in Giles County, Virginia; on the AT north of Doyle River Parking Area and Big Meadows in SNP; and in the upland forests of Catoctin Mountain Park in Maryland.

TYROL KNAPWEED

Centaurea nigrescens

FLOWER:
The one-inch flower heads are composed entirely of pinkish-purple disk (no ray) flowers that grow at the end of loosely arranged branches. The outer ones are larger than the inner ones.

LEAVES AND STEM:
The leaves that grow on the lower portion of the one to three foot stem are divided into fingerlike lobes, with those near the top being larger, simple, and not divided.

BLOOM SEASON:
June to September

The casual observer may mistake Tyrol Knapweed for one of the Thistles, such as the Bull Thistle (*Cirsium vulgare;* see page 190). A closer examination will show that the Tyrol Knapweed has a smooth stem and leaves as opposed to the bristles found on the Thistles. In addition, the Thistles' flower heads are generally more dense.

Both flowers grow in fields, roadsides, and waste areas, and belong to the Composite family, whose members include Yarrow (*Achillea millefolium;* see page 60), Common Burdock (*Arctium minus;* see page 202), and White Snakeroot (*Eupatorium rugosum;* see page 94).

The common name of Knapweed is a derivative of the German word *kobbe,* which means "button" and refers to the shape of the flower head. In fact, another common name is Bachelor's Button. The genus name of *Centaurea* is for Chiron the Centaur, who supposedly used one of the plants to cure a wound that was accidentally received from one of Hercules' poisoned arrows. (Some stories say that it was a Gentian and not a Knapweed that was used.)

One of the other Knapweeds you may find growing in the Blue Ridge and Great Smoky Mountains is Spotted Knapweed (*Centaurea maculosa*), whose species name of *maculosa* translates to "spotted" and refers to the black tips on the leaf bracts at the base of the flowers. When looking to other sources for further information on Spotted Knapweed, you should be aware some reference books list it as *Centaurea biebersteinii.*

Some places you may find one of the Knapweeds include: BRP mileposts 78.4, 89, 95.4, 110.9, 139, 154.1, 235, 236.9, and 240.9; and Southwest Virginia Agricultural Research and Extension Center off Hillman Highway between Glade Spring and Emory, Virginia.

WILD BERGAMOT

Monarda fistulosa

Wild Bergamot is a member of the mint family and, as such, has been used as a scent in perfumes and as a flavoring in cooking. Growing in thickets and open meadows and along woodland borders, colonies of the plant are conspicuous; their tall stems, which tower above much of the other undergrowth, are topped by rich pink to lavender tubular flowers.

Although bees are attracted to the flower, the long floral tubes—which make it hard for insects to reach the nectar—are more suited to the bills of hummingbirds, who are probably the plant's primary pollinators. Yet, just as with Squirrel Corn (*Dicentra canadensis;* see page 22), Spotted Jewelweed (*Impatiens capensis;* see page 252), Columbine (*Aquilegia canadensis;* see page 168), and Trumpet Vine (*Campsis radicans;* see page 194), insects whose tongues are too short or bodies too large to gain access to the nectar by crawling into the tubes have learned that all they have to do is nip the tip to get a taste of the syrupy liquid.

Tea made from the leaves has the same antiseptic compounds found in commercial breath fresheners such as Listerine, so it is a good choice for those plagued by halitosis. In addition, it contains geranoil, a compound proven to prevent tooth decay.

Wild Bergamot is also commonly called Lavender Bergamot and Horse Mint, a name often applied to all members of the genus, such as Bee Balm (*Monarda didyma;* see page 196) and Dotted Monarda (*Monarda punctata*).

Some places you may encounter Wild Bergamot include: BRP mileposts 38.8, 78.4, 260.3, 308.2, 339.5, 368–374, 417, and 432.7; along Haymakertown Road (VA 600) in Botetourt County, House Mountain Trail near Lexington, and Turkey Roost and Hawk Creek Trails at Lake Robertson, also near Lexington, Virginia; and in the lower elevations of Catoctin Mountain Park in Maryland.

FLOWER:
  Occurring in a terminal cluster, the individual pink to lavender flowers are one inch long and have an ascending, hairy upper lip with a broader, three-lobed drooping lower lip.

LEAVES AND STEM:
  The two- to three-inch gray-green leaves are quite toothed and grow oppositely along the length of the two- to four-foot stem.

BLOOM SEASON:
  June to September

WILD BASIL

Satureja vulgaris

FLOWER:
The reddish-violet (sometimes almost white) flowers are tubular with the corolla having two lips. The flowers are arranged in rounded, woolly-looking clusters that grow from the axils of the upper leaves.

LEAVES AND STEM:
The one- to one-and-a-half-inch, egg-shaped leaves are sometimes toothed and grow opposite on the six-inch to two-foot, slightly hairy stem.

BLOOM SEASON:
June to September

Although the two are related and are members of the Mint family, Wild Basil is not the spice you add to make your spaghetti sauce more flavorful. Wild Basil's leaves can be used as a seasoning, but most people who have sampled them say they impart more of a flavor of Thyme than of Basil.

Like most mints, Wild Basil has a square stem that will help you identify it, but if you look to other books for more information, you will find that it has a number of other common names, such as Field Basil, Cushion Calamint, Hedge Calamint, Hedge Basil, Summer Savory, Dog Mint, and Borstelkrans. In addition, some references list it as *Clinopodium vulgare. Clinopodium* means "bedfoot," which some observers say refers to how the plant's terminal clusters resemble the knobs on the foot of a bed frame.

The common name is derived from the Greek word *basilikos,* meaning "royal," and is said to be a reference to the rich taste and smell of the plant, attributes that make it fit for a king's palate.

Most authorities agree that Wild Basil only grew in the more northern parts of North America when early settlers began to arrive from Europe. The plants now found in the Blue Ridge and Great Smoky Mountains are not the result of the species naturally migrating southward, but rather are the descendants of plants and seeds that were imported from Europe.

Look for Wild Basil in open meadows, along roadsides, in sunny woodlands, and in thickets.

Some places you may encounter Wild Basil include: BRP mileposts 51.7 and 252.8.

189

BULL THISTLE

Cirsium vulgare

The flower heads are one-and-a-half to two inches across and have numerous purple flowers.

The leaves, which are pinnately divided and have prickly wings running down from their bases, grow alternately on stems that could reach six feet high.

June to September

Close to twenty species of Thistle grow in the eastern United States and all but a few have leaves that you don't want to brush up against. In addition to this, the plants can become a real problem once they invade a grazing field. Cattle, of course, shun the prickly foliage, which spreads to take over much of the acreage.

Despite this nasty reputation, the Thistles are beneficial in a number of ways. The leaves and stems can be a nutritious livestock feed once they have been ground up and the thorns removed. Bees make a honey from the nectar that many people consider a rare treat, while the flowers have been used to make a fragrant wine. Birds are attracted to the seeds in such great numbers that some people are willing to pay a premium price so that they can include the seeds in their bird feeders.

Hairy stems and two- to three-inch flower heads are characteristic of Pasture Thistle (*Cirsium pumilum*). Fine white hairs grow underneath the leaves of Field Thistle (*Cirsium dicolor*), while the stem is smooth. The leaves of Tall Thistle (*Cirsium altissimum*) are unlobed but have large teeth.

When looking to other sources for further information on the Thistles, you should be aware some reference books place them within the genus *Cardus*.

Some places you may encounter one of the Thistles include: Heintooga Ridge Road in GSMNP; BRP mileposts 235.8, 240.9, and 277.9; on the AT north of Doyle River Parking Area in SNP; Lake Trail at Lake Robertson near Lexington, and Chessie Nature Trail in Rockbridge County, Virginia; and in Big Meadows in SNP.

OBEDIENT PLANT

Physostegia virginiana

This may be one of the showiest members of the Mint family. Its long, tubular flowers recall those of the Snapdragons (hence, another common name, False Dragonhead), and when the sun shines through them it highlights their rich pink veins, bringing to mind the delicate beauty of the Pink Lady's Slippers (*Cypripedium acaule;* see page 254). The tubes are also spotted with bits of purple; four stamens grow inside. The lowest flowers bloom first, with the process proceeding upward along the stem. Each flower is attached to the stem by a short stalk and a green calyx with five pointed teeth.

Botanists theorize that the reason the flowers are clustered so tightly together is to prevent certain insects, such as wasps, from eating a hole in the base of the tube to obtain the nectar without brushing against the flower's reproductive parts and helping fertilize the plant.

Like most Mints, the Obedient Plant has a square stem, but the easiest way for you to identify it will also teach you how it received its common name. Gently push the flowers to the left or the right and they will not immediately return to their original position but will "obediently" stay in place for quite some time.

With close to 200 genera and more than 3,000 species, the Mints are found almost everywhere in the world. Among those that you are probably most familiar with, and may use almost daily, are Thyme, Basil, Oregano, Marjoram, Sage, and Catnip.

Some places you may encounter Obedient Plant include moist areas of the lower elevations of GSMNP and BRP milepost 461.

TRUMPET VINE

Campsis radicans

FLOWER:
  Borne in terminal clusters, the flaring, trumpet-shaped flowers have five lobes and are three inches long.

LEAVES AND STEM:
  The paired leaves are divided into five to seven ovate, toothed leaflets, each two to three inches long. This is a creeping vine that can grow to twenty feet.

BLOOM SEASON:
  July to September

Trumpet Vine, also known as Cow Itch because it can cause contact dermatitis, grows along road edges and woodland borders. Aerial roots coming from the stem enable the plant to creep (thus, another common name, Trumpet Creeper) and climb over and upon other vegetation, sometimes becoming so aggressive and well established that it can be a nuisance plant. Other names, such as Devil's Shoestrings and Hellvine, reflect this propensity. The leaves you see will usually have been produced within the last two years, as the older parts of the plant become leafless and woody. The original portion of the stem may grow to a half foot in diameter, and its bark may become fissured like that of a tree.

An inhabitant of the lowlands, the Trumpet Vine has distinctive reddish-orange blossoms that are attractive to ruby-throated hummingbirds, one of the plant's primary pollinators. In fact, the bird is of such importance to the Trumpet Vine's reproductive cycle that its natural range almost mirrors that of the hummingbird.

When the bird sticks its beak deep into the flower to reach the nectar located at the base of the "trumpet," its head becomes dusted with pollen as it grazes against the anthers. Repeating the movement at the next blossom it visits, the bird deposits the pollen onto the pistil, thereby insuring pollination. It has been observed that the hummingbird sometimes cheats the flower by poking a hole in the calyx and drinking the nectar without fertilizing the plants.

Some places you may encounter Trumpet Vine include: GA 136 in Walker County, Georgia; west of the site of Reid's Lock on the Chessie Nature Trail between Lexington and Buena Vista, Virginia; and the C&O Canal Towpath in Maryland.

BEE BALM

Monarda didyma

FLOWER:
The individual bright red flowers of the Bee Balm are about one-and-a-half inches long and have an ascending upper lip with a broader, drooping lower lip.

LEAVES AND STEM:
The three- to six-inch dark green leaves are quite toothed and grow in pairs along the length of the two- to four-foot stem.

BLOOM SEASON:
July to September

Bee Balm inhabits moist areas in woodlands and beside streams, ponds, and lakes where it is often seen growing close to the Cardinal Flower (*Lobelia cardinalis;* see page 198). The rich, scarlet red of both blossoms, which last throughout much of the summer, attract ruby-throated hummingbirds, the only hummingbirds found in the Blue Ridge and Great Smoky Mountains. They are also the only birds in the world that are known to fly backward; their wings beat so fast that they appear to be no more than a blur. Evidently their feeding is as frenzied as their flight; their tongues slurp up nectar at the amazing rate of eighteen licks per second.

Bee Balm is also called Oswego Tea for the Oswego Indians of New York, who made a drink from the leaves to ease the symptoms of fevers and chills. Other common names include Indian Plume, Mountain Mint, and Fragrant Balm. The genus name *Monarda* honors Nicolas Monardes, a physician and naturalist who lived in Seville, Spain, and published *Joyfull Newes Out of the Newe Founde Worlde,* a sixteenth-century text on the medicinal values of plants newly discovered in North America. The species name, *didyma,* is Greek for "pairs." One source states that this name refers to the way the leaves grow in twos along the stems, while another claims that it indicates that each flower has pairs of stamens.

Some places you may encounter Bee Balm include: Green Ridge Trail in Madison County, North Carolina; Kanati Fork Trail, Chimneys Picnic Area, and Clingmans Dome Road in GSMNP; BRP mileposts 26.3 and 316.5; on the AT next to Brown Mountain Creek in central Virginia, and across the footbridge leading from the AT to Fuller Lake Beach in Pine Grove Furnace State Park in Pennsylvania; Mount Rogers Trail in Smyth County, Virginia; and Skyline Drive milepost 75.2 in SNP.

CARDINAL FLOWER

Lobelia cardinalis

The brilliant red flowers grow in a long cluster, are about one-and-a-half inches long, and have five petals that form two lips; the upper one has two lobes while the lower one has three spreading lobes. The stamens are united in a tube around the single pistil.

The lanceolate leaves average six inches in length, are irregularly toothed, and grow alternately on the two- to five-foot stem.

July to September

The web of life is an amazing thing that seems to have no end to its number of strands. In addition to propagating by seeds, the Cardinal Flower sends out shoots that rise above the ground as a rosette of leaves. The following year, the rosette matures into a flowering plant that sends out its own shoots. To obtain the strength needed to accomplish this, the basal leaves stay green year round, gathering nourishment through photosynthesis. This is why the Cardinal Flower grows close to streams; it depends on these waterways to overflow their banks every so often and clear away any litter or debris on the leaves that block the amount of sunlight reaching them. So, whenever human beings change the natural flow of rivers and creeks, they affect the health and life of the Cardinal Flower.

The genus name *Lobelia* honors French botanist Matthias de l'Obel. A story that has passed down through many generations of flower lovers (and yet is hard to verify) provides the origin of the plant's common and species names. Upon being presented with a new plant sent from North America, French queen Henrietta Maria, wife of King Charles I, is said to have sniggered at it because its color reminded her of the stockings and robes worn by Catholic cardinals.

Some places you may encounter Cardinal Flower include: Chattahoochee Nature Center in Roswell, Georgia; Schoolhouse Gap Trail, and Cades Cove Loop and Tremont Roads in GSMNP; on the AT near Laurel Falls in Tennessee, south side of Poor Valley in southwest Virginia, Johns Hollow in central Virginia, and Pine Grove Furnace State Park in Pennsylvania; Pandapas Pond Trail in Montgomery County, and Ivy Creek Natural Area near Charlottesville, Virginia; and in the lower elevations of Catoctin Mountain Park, and south of Right Hand Fork Road on the Catoctin Trail in Frederick County, Maryland.

DENSE
BLAZING STAR

Liatris spicata

FLOWER:
   Densely clustered along a tall spike to which they are attached without stalks, the flower heads are only a quarter of an inch wide. Each one has numerous long styles that extend beyond the petals and each flower head is supported by purple-tinged, scaly bracts.

LEAVES AND STEM:
   Like the flowers, the narrow leaves are crowded along the one- to six-foot stem. The lower leaves are about a foot long; the upper ones get progressively smaller.

BLOOM SEASON:
   July to September

The Dense Blazing Star is one of the prettiest of the late-summer and fall flowers, its tall spikes of purple-rose blossoms accenting the other vegetation of the bogs, wet meadows, moist open woods, and rocky slopes that it inhabits. The flowers mature from the top to the bottom, unlike most spiked plants. The flowers' elongated styles give the spikes a light feathery appearance, earning the plant the common name Gay Feather.

Of course, like many other plants, it does not have only one or two common names. The name Marsh Blazing Star obviously derives from the moist environment that the plants need in order to grow. Rattlesnake Master and Button Snakeroot both refer to the fact that Native Americans used the plant to treat snakebites. The latter name also describes the button-like appearance of the plant's tuberous, bulb-shaped root, which was sometimes stored for winter food.

Mothers used to make a tea from the root to treat colicky babies, while a liniment made with the root and alcohol was rubbed on sore backs and muscles.

Several other Blazing Stars inhabit the area; unfortunately they hybridize so easily that it may be hard to tell one species from another. Grass-Leaved Blazing Star (*Liatris graminifolia*) has a hairy stem and sometimes has branched flower clusters, while the lowest leaves of the Large Blazing Star (*Liatris scariosa*) are almost one-and-a-half inches wide and are attached to the stem by long stalks.

Some places you may encounter one of the Blazing Stars include: BRP mileposts 305.1 and 369–370; on the AT near Johns Hollow Shelter in central Virginia; and Lewis Falls Trail in SNP.

200

COMMON BURDOCK

Arctium minus

Originally found in Europe and Asia, Common Burdock is one of those pesky plants that attaches parts of itself to you and your clothing when you walk by it in an overgrown field or along a road. Of course, you can't blame the plant; all it is trying to do is spread its seed. Barbed bracts located below the flower head are designed to snag animal fur so that the seeds will eventually fall off far from the parent plant. What can be even more annoying is that this burr breaks apart when you try to pick it off. Again, this is by design so that the seeds will be deposited on the ground bit by bit and not all at once.

Despite being such bothersome plants, members of the *Arctium* genus have had a long history of medicinal use. Europeans prescribed various concoctions for fever, acne, gonorrhea, ringworm, gout, dandruff, and more. Americans in the 1800s used the plants as a diuretic and a treatment for kidney problems and urinary tract infections.

Today, researchers have found that fresh *Arctium* roots contain polyacetylenes, chemicals that kill disease-causing fungi and bacteria. An article in the magazine *Chemotherapy* stated that the plant inhibited tumor growth in experiments, while *Mutation Research* reported that Burdock decreased mutations in cells that had been exposed to possible cancer-causing chemicals. In *The Green Pharmacy,* Dr. James A. Duke presents a recipe for what he calls gobo gumbo (*gobo* is Japanese for "burdock") that uses one cup of fresh Burdock stem because he says that the plant's juices and extracts "show test-tube activity against HIV."

Some places you may encounter Common Burdock include: along the carriage trails of Moses Cone Memorial Park at BRP mileposts 294–295.4; and on US 58 between Grayson Highlands State Park and Damascus, Virginia.

TURTLEHEAD

Chelone lyonii

FLOWER:
  *Growing in narrow, dense termi-
nal clusters, the one-inch flowers are
actually five petals that have fused
together to form a two-lipped tube.*

LEAVES AND STEM:
  *The ovate three- to seven-inch
leaves are sharply toothed, have slender stems more than an inch long,
and grow oppositely along the one-
to two-foot stem.*

BLOOM SEASON:
  Late July to early October

Do not be alarmed if you find yourself walking beside a blossom that appears to be moving about on its own accord and whose flesh is slightly rippling. You have not discovered a flower that has jumped the barrier from plant to animal life. Hang around a few moments and you will see a bee that has been in search of nectar emerge from the floral tube of the Turtlehead. Having forced its way in by parting the upper and lower lips, the insect has not only enjoyed a sip of nectar but has also brushed against the anthers. The pollen from these male organs will be deposited on the female organ of the next blossom the bee forces its way into.

The flower is aptly named, as the upper lip certainly looks like the top of a turtle's head (the genus name is from the Greek for "tortoise"). The inflated throat is woolly inside and tinged with a contrasting yellow hue, while the lower lip has three curled lobes that act as an insect landing pad. The species name *lyonii* is for John Lyon, a nineteenth-century American botanist.

The White Turtlehead (*Chelone glabra*) has white flow-ers, while the leaves of the Red, or Purple, Turtlehead (*Chelone obliqua*) are smaller with shorter stalks. The rarer Cuthbert's Turtlehead (*Chelone cuthbertii*) has sessile leaves and dark lines on the inside of the flower's lower lip.

Some places you may encounter one of the Turtleheads include: Mount LeConte, Clingmans Dome Road, and Alum Cave and Boulevard Trails in GSMNP; BRP mile-posts 304.7, 365.4, and 451.2; on the AT between Big Meadows and Fishers Gap Overlook in SNP; and Pearl Thompson Creek on Forest Service Road 201 in Giles County, and Henry Lanum Trail in Nelson County, Virginia.

TALL IRONWEED

Vernonia gigantea

In moist fields, thickets, stream banks, and roadsides, the blossoms of Ironweed join those of the Asters, Daisies, and Goldenrods as waning daylight hours usher late summer into fall. Once known as *Vernonia altissima,* the common name of Ironweed refers to its tough, rigid stem, an attribute cursed by farmers when they find out how hard this weed is to cut and remove from a grazing field.

The genus name *Vernonia* was given to the plant in tribute to William Vernon, a late-1600s English botanist who traveled to North America to explore its diverse vegetation. *Altissima,* the species name, obviously pertains to the height the plant attains.

Native Americans made a tea from the leaves to treat ailments and illnesses ranging from sore throats to stomach ulcers to the pains of childbirth. An infusion made from the roots was thought to help alleviate symptoms of pneumonia and treat snakebites. In addition, some people believed that holding the root tea in their mouth for an extended period would help tighten teeth and keep them from falling out.

New York Ironweed (*Vernonia noveboracensis*), which may grow three to six feet tall, has bracts that are feathery, not pointed; leaves that are narrower; and as many as fifty individual flowers in its clusters.

Some places you may encounter Ironweed include: Harper Valley Road off the Foothills Parkway near Chilhowee, Tennessee; along the Cades Cove Loop Road in GSMNP; BRP mileposts 17.6, 162.4, 231.8, 245, and 248; and within the first mile of the Hotel Trail in Nelson County, Virginia.

206

VIRGINIA BLUEBELL

Mertensia virginica

FLOWER:
About an inch long, the funnel-shaped flower is actually five fused petals. The ends flare out like the bell of a trumpet.

LEAVES AND STEM:
The blue-green basal leaves are about six inches long, with the other leaves getting progressively smaller as they grow alternately up the one- to two-foot, smooth, fleshy stem.

BLOOM SEASON:
March to June

Reflecting the clarity of an early spring sky, the blossoms of the Virginia Bluebell can add an unexpected elegance to the shaded stream banks and moist bottomlands in which they grow. Pink when they first appear as buds, the flowers develop into nodding clusters of bright, light blue trumpets. Some people have described the color as "china dish" or "porcelain" blue. They often grow in large colonies, but be sure to get out and see them in early spring: once the flowers mature and the seeds develop, all aboveground evidence of the plant disappears.

Also commonly known as Virginia Cowslip, Roanoke Bells, and Mertensia, Virginia Bluebell is a far-ranging plant that is found not only in the Blue Ridge and Great Smoky Mountains but also as far north as Ontario, Canada, and as far west as the Ozark Mountains of Missouri and Arkansas. It is a member of the Forget-me-not family, which contains about 100 genera and 2,000 species, including Viper's Bugloss (*Echium vulgare;* see page 230).

Named for German botanist Franz Karl Mertens, who lived from 1764 to 1831, some members of the genus *Mertensia* are also known as Lungworts because it was once believed that they could be used as a cure for diseases of the lung. But this has never been proven, and the plant has no history of any other medicinal uses.

Some places you may encounter Virginia Bluebell include: The Pocket on Pigeon Mountain in Walker County, Georgia; and Haymakertown Road (VA 600) in Botetourt County, and the Chessie Nature Trail in Rockbridge County, Virginia.

BIRDSFOOT VIOLET

Viola pedata

More than an inch wide, the blue-violet flowers have five petals, with the lower petals often being larger than the others.

Rising from short, fleshy root-stocks, the leaves are fan-shaped and cut into many deeply lobed segments.

Late March to June

One of the largest members of the Violet family, the Birdsfoot Violet is easy to identify because its leaves form a distinctive "bird's foot" pattern. The conspicuous orange anthers at the end of the stamens in the flower's throat add a touch of brilliance. Even prettier is a bicolored form often found throughout the Blue Ridge and Great Smoky Mountains. Its upper petals are a rich violet, while there is a lighter lilac hue to the lower ones.

However, violets are not just pretty flowers. Euell Gibbons, author of *Stalking the Wild Asparagus* and possibly America's foremost proponent of wild foods, called the flowers nature's vitamin pill, as the leaves and blossoms contain high amounts of vitamins A and C. The flowers may be eaten raw; some people have used them to make a fragrant and tasty jelly.

A story of love, jealousy, and anger that resolves happily tells the origin of the Violet: Zeus fell in love with a woodland nymph named Io. In retaliation, his wife Hera turned Io into a cow, who wept in sorrow at her fate. Wherever her tears fell, beautiful Violets began to grow. Eventually, Zeus was able to secretly take Io to Egypt where, away from Hera's watchful eye, the lovely nymph was restored to her former self.

Some places you may encounter Birdsfoot Violet include: Tallulah Falls State Park in Georgia; along Rich Mountain Road and Cooper Road Trail in GSMNP; BRP mileposts 147.4, 202, 260.5, and 379; on the AT on Catawba Mountain and near Johns Hollow Shelter in central Virginia; Nature Conservancy Trail in Giles County, and Sky Meadows State Park in Virginia; Old Rag in SNP; and Green Ridge Hiking Trail in Allegany County, Maryland.

CRESTED
DWARF IRIS

Iris cristata

FLOWER:

The pale to deep purple flowers are divided into six parts. The three petals are narrow and arching, while the three petal-like sepals are broader, curve downward, are streaked with purple, and are "crested" with white to yellow ridges.

LEAVES AND STEM:

The lance-shaped leaves are a half to an inch wide, sheath the three- to eight-inch stem, and may grow to twelve inches in length.

BLOOM SEASON:

April to May

While its much larger relative, the Blue Flag Iris (*Iris versicolor;* see page 222), can be very noticeable, growing three feet tall in ditches, ponds, and wet meadows, the diminutive Crested Dwarf Iris may be hidden by the vegetative litter that accumulates on the forest floor where it grows. You may overlook it, but insects that insure its propagation don't. In their search for food, they brush against the styles that conceal the pollen-laden anthers. Moving to the next flower, they fertilize the plant as they repeat the process.

Native Americans made an ointment from the roots by mixing it with animal fat to rub on skin ulcers; a tea from the root has been prescribed by herbalists to treat hepatitis. Edward Lewis Sturtevant, the first director of the New York Agricultural Station, wrote in his *Edible Plants of the World,* published in the early 1900s, that chewing on the root produced a sweet taste that soon turned into a burning sensation. (Which surely begs the question, who did this and did they continue to do it?) He also claimed that doing this could alleviate thirst.

Dwarf Iris (*Iris verna*) does not have the white to yellow "crest" ridge on its flowers' outer segments, and its leaves are narrower and more grasslike.

Some places you may encounter one of the Dwarf Irises include: Deep Creek and Joyce Kilmer Memorial Trails in Joyce Kilmer–Slickrock Wilderness in North Carolina; Little River Gorge, and Roaring Fork Motor Nature, Porters Creek, and Bradley Fork Trails in GSMNP; BRP mileposts 110.7, 195, 198, 210, 217, 250.8, 273.4, and 379; and on the AT between Springer Mountain and Neel's Gap in Georgia, near Bear Wallow Gap in central Virginia, and Michaux State Forest in Pennsylvania.

WILD BLUE PHLOX

Phlox divaricata

Growing in a loose cluster, the one-and-a-half-inch, pale blue to light purple flowers are actually five petals that have united to form a slender tube that ends in five spreading, notched lobes.

The one- to two-inch sessile leaves grow in pairs that are widely spaced along the eight- to twenty-inch slightly sticky stem.

April to June

A quick glance at the clusters of flowers growing on the many-branched stems of the Wild Blue Phlox reveals the origin of the species name *divaricata,* which is Latin for "divergent" or "branched." But what about the genus name *Phlox,* from the Greek word for "flame"? You must be a very dedicated wildflower watcher and monitor the plant to catch it just as the blossoms are beginning to form. It is at this time, before they open, that the buds are a tightly wound spiral that reminded some observers of the flames on the torches carried by the ancient Greeks.

Once Wild Blue Phlox, also commonly called Wild Sweet William (a name also applied to the species *Phlox maculata*), has opened, look inside the floral tube and you will see that the short stamens are hidden inside, while the long pistil with three stigmas extends well beyond the end of the tube. Interestingly, while the lobes of the flowers found in the Smokies and Blue Ridge are notched, those of the same species that grow in the western part of the country are not.

Among the other species that inhabit the Blue Ridge and Great Smoky Mountains is Creeping Phlox (*Phlox stolonifera*). It often grows close to Wild Blue Phlox and trails across the ground to send up stalks with rose-purple flowers whose stamens and pistils both extend beyond the floral tube. Garden Phlox (*Phlox paniculata*) is the familiar culti-vated species that may grow up to six feet tall.

Some places you may encounter a Phlox include: Sloppy Floyd State Park in Georgia; Newfound Gap and Little River Roads, and Porters Creek Trail in GSMNP; BRP mileposts 4, 79–82, 163–164, 200–202, 219–221, 339.3, 370–380, 411, and 432.7; and the Cascades Trail in Giles County, Virginia.

SPIDERWORT

Tradescantia virginiana

*The violet flowers grow in a ter-
minal cluster, each having three
rounded petals from which spring six
hairy, yellowish-gold stamens.*

*The fifteen-inch, iris-like leaves
are folded lengthwise and grow oppositely on a one- to two-foot-high
stem.*

April to July

Spiderwort is found in a variety of environments—in ditches and meadows, on roadsides, along woodlands, and in thickets and forests—throughout the region. Many people find it so appealing that they include it in their wildflower gardens.

However, the plant has so many different attributes that it has piqued the interest of scientists in a variety of fields. Botanists investigate its genetic makeup because it appears to be a link between the simple Sedges and the more advanced Lilies. The hairs on the stamens are composed of thin-walled cells, enabling easy microscopic examinations of the cytoplasm and nucleus. This research may one day aid in the treatment of abnormalities and malignancies in human cells. (These researchers must be careful in handling the plant, as the sap contains raphides, irritating needle-shaped crystals of calcium oxalate.) Other scientists have found that parts of the plant change color when exposed to radiation and other types of pollution and are now using the Spiderwort as a monitoring tool.

A limp, mucilaginous thread—about as fine as a spider's web—can be pulled from the jointed stems but quickly hardens when exposed to the air. On the other hand, the flower, which lasts only one day after being fertilized, has an enzyme that causes it to dissolve into a runny, gelatinous blob—earning the plant another name, Widow's Tears.

Zigzag Spiderwort (*Tradescantia subaspera*) has a zigzagging stem and blue flowers, and Ohio Spiderwort (*Tradescantia ohiensis*) has flowers ranging from blue to light red.

Some places you may encounter one of the Spiderworts include: Chunky Gal Trail in Clay County, North Carolina; Round Bottom Road and Noland Divide Trail in GSMNP; BRP mileposts 290.5, 308.2, and 457.9; and Skyline Drive mileposts 57.5 to 60.2 in SNP.

HEAL-ALL

Prunella vulgaris

Like Wild Basil (*Satureja vulgaris;* see page 188), another member of the Mint family, Heal-All is so prevalent (the species name *vulgaris* means common) and such a small flower of fields, roadsides, and front lawns that it is often overlooked. This is a shame, for it has some of the richest violet to blue hues to be found anywhere.

Its shape is also one of the most interesting you will see. The upper lip, which has tiny hairs on top, is indented and bent over to provide a protective hood for the lower, drooping lip. Looking straight at the blossom will bring to mind the head of a science-fiction creature, as if you're staring right into its open mouth, its jagged teeth and deep throat exposed!

With a name like Heal-All, also known as Self-Heal, the plant has, of course, been believed to have many medicinal powers. Based on the Doctrine of Signatures, it was often prescribed to treat ailments of the mouth and throat, including tonsillitis. In fact, the genus name *Prunella* is based on the German word *brunella,* meaning "throat inflammation."

The plant is also an effective astringent that helps slow the flow of blood and heal wounds. There are some indications that Heal-All has antibacterial and anticancer properties, and near the turn of the twenty-first century, Canadian researchers obtained a substance from Heal-All that shows promise in fighting herpes.

Some places you may encounter Heal-All include: Newfound Gap Road and Bradley Fork Trail in GSMNP; BRP mileposts 243, 277.9, 308.2, and 411; on the AT at Three Forks in Georgia; Crest and Fairwood Valley Trails in Smyth County, Virginia; and throughout Catoctin Mountain Park in Maryland.

BLUE-EYED GRASS
Sisyrinchium
angustifolium

FLOWER:

The half-inch, rich violet-blue flower with a yellow center has three petals and three sepals (that are similar to the petals). All are tipped with a small point.

LEAVES AND STEM:

The grasslike leaves that branch in two from the stem and have two wings are less than a quarter-inch wide and, at four to twenty inches in height, may be shorter or taller than the flower stalks.

BLOOM SEASON:

May to July

Despite its common name, this is not a grass, but the smallest member of the Iris family—and one of Henry David Thoreau's favorite wildflowers. Like those of the Wild Geranium (*Geranium maculatum;* see page 158), the flowers of Blue-Eyed Grass have dark blue lines that help guide bees and other insects to the plant's nectar, pollen, and reproductive parts. It is also commonly called Stout Blue-Eyed Grass. Another name is Narrow-Leaved Blue-Eyed Grass, which is what its species name, *angustifolium,* means.

Sisyrinchium, the genus name, is from the Greek for "pig (or hog) snout" and was given to the plant because wild pigs eat the roots and will dig up large patches of ground to get to them. (See Spring Beauty [*Claytonia virginica;* page 152] for a discussion about wild boars' damage in Great Smoky Mountains National Park.)

Found in open areas, on roads, and in moist woodlands, there are several species of Blue-Eyed Grass in the region, but the differences among them are slight and identification may be difficult. Slender Blue-Eyed Grass (*Sisyrinchium mucronatum*) does not have a branching stem, while the stems of Eastern Blue-Eyed Grass (*Sisyrinchium atlanticum*) are barely two-winged. You may be able to pick out White Blue-Eyed Grass (*Sisyrinchium albidum*) because its flowers are sometime white (but, then again, they are sometimes blue).

Some places you may encounter Blue-Eyed Grass include: Hooper Bald along the Cherohala Skyway in North Carolina; Little River Gorge, Heintooga Ridge, and Cades Cove Loop Roads, and The Boulevard Trail in GSMNP; BRP mileposts 229.7, 290.5, and 303.7; and on the AT north of Newfound Gap in GSMNP.

BLUE FLAG IRIS

Iris versicolor

Resembling larger versions of the Crested Dwarf Iris (*Iris cristata;* see page 212), Blue Flag Iris is not found as often as it once was because highways, housing developments, and shopping areas have been constructed in the wetlands and moist fields it prefers. However, since the plant reproduces both from seeds and from its creeping rhizomes, where you find one flower you often find an entire colony.

Although the root contains a strong poison, Native Americans used it for stomach and intestinal complaints, as a laxative, and as a poultice on wounds. In what may be good news to overweight Americans, researchers have found that the plant produces a substance that increases the metabolism, helping the body convert fat into waste. (Iris has been used in India for decades to help people lose unwanted pounds.)

Around 1500 B.C., Thutmose III included the Iris on the wall of his temple in Karnak, while Clovis I, King of the Franks around 500 A.D., took the flower as his emblem. When Louis VII included the flower on his banner, it became known as the fleur-de-lis, the "Flower of Louis," and was used as a symbol of France's victory in the Second Crusade.

Despite this use on a number of royal banners, the "flag" in the plant's common name refers to its leaves' resembling those of the Reeds, whose English name was once "flagge." Since the plants grow in such densely packed colonies, the narrowness of the leaves and the way they grow vertically instead of horizontally—in addition to being able to assimilate light on both sidesof the leaf—enables them to soak up more sunlight than broad-leafed plants do.

Some places you may encounter Blue Flag Iris include: Chattahoochee Nature Center in Roswell, Georgia; and BRP mileposts 162.4 and 230.1.

PROSTRATE BLUETS

Houstonia serpyllifolia

Four light blue to almost white petals are joined at a slightly yellow center. Each stem, which creeps along the ground before becoming erect, has a single flower.

Leaves are opposite and mostly basal on a two- to eight-inch stem.

May to August

Like the Virginia Bluebells (*Mertensia virginica;* see page 208), the pale blue Prostrate Bluets, also commonly called Thyme-Leaved Bluets, reflect the purity of an early spring sky. In fact, the species name is Latin for "sky blue." *Houstonia,* the genus name, honors William Houston, a ship's surgeon who collected plants (although not Bluets) and kept extensive notes during his travels throughout the Caribbean in the 1700s.

Among the many species of Bluets that grow in the region are Long-Leaved Bluets (*Houstonia longifolia*), with terminal clusters of two or three, white to pale purple flowers, and Large or Mountain Houstonia (*Houstonia purpurea*), which has ribbed leaves that grow oppositely on a four- to eighteen-inch stem and white or pink flowers that grow in terminal clusters. *Houstonia caerulea,* often referred to simply as Common Bluets, is very similar to Prostrate Bluets, except its stems do not creep along the ground and its flowers bloom from April to early July.

Fertilized by small butterflies, such as Clouded Sulphurs, Fritillaries, and Painted Ladies, the Bluets are known by a number of common names including Innocence, Quaker Maids, Little Washerwomen, and Venus's Pride. The name Eyebright refers to the patch of yellow in the center of each flower.

Some places you may encounter one of the Bluets include: Newfound Gap, Clingmans Dome, and Balsam Mountain Roads, and The Boulevard Trail in GSMNP; BRP mileposts 200.2, 305, 355–368, 421.7, and 451.2; on the AT between Springer Mountain and Neels Gap in Georgia, between Deep Gap and Wallace Gap in North Carolina, and Humpback Mountain in central Virginia; North River Gorge Trail in Augusta County, Virginia; lower elevations of Old Rag in SNP; and the north end of Green Ridge Hiking Trail in Allegany County, Maryland.

HORSE NETTLE

Solanum carolinense

The five-lobed, lavender to white flowers are almost an inch wide and have protruding yellow anthers that form a cone or "beak" in the middle of the blossom.

The branched, prickly stem grows one to three feet tall and has three-to five-inch, coarsely lobed, prickly leaves.

May to October

Although it has clusters of appealing, star-shaped flowers, Horse Nettle can become a nuisance for farmers and ranchers. Also known as Bull Nettle, Apple-of-Sodom, and Sandbrier, it is a perennial whose stems are covered with sharp thorns. It can quickly saturate a meadow, as it is not eaten by livestock and its deep-growing roots make it hard to destroy. When walking through a meadow at the end of the growing season, you will see this plant's tiny, yellow, tomato-like fruits hanging onto withering tan branches and foliage.

In fact, Horse Nettle and tomatoes are related and are members of the Nightshade family, which also includes potatoes, chilies, bell peppers, and eggplants. Be aware, though, that Horse Nettle's fruit is poisonous to humans, especially children. Some animals and birds eat the fruits without ill effect.

Native Americans soothed sore throats by gargling with a tea made from the leaves, drank it to treat worms, and applied it to the skin to relieve the itch of poison ivy. The plant has also been used as an antispasmodic for those afflicted with epilepsy, bronchitis, and asthma.

Solanum dulcamara, commonly called Bittersweet Nightshade or Climbing Nightshade, grows throughout the Blue Ridge and Great Smoky Mountains and is a creeping vine with clusters of drooping, rich purple or blue, star-shaped flowers. Its fruit is green when it first appears, but matures to a bright red, making it look very much like the commercially sold grape tomatoes.

Some places you may encounter Horse Nettle include: roads in Floyd County, Georgia; Little River Road in GSMNP; and BRP mileposts 244.7, 252.8, 277.9, 281.5, 290.5, 337.2, 399.7, and 467.8.

TALL BELLFLOWER

Campanula americana

FLOWER:

Growing from the axils of leaflike bracts along the stem, the blue flowers have five petals that form a star with a white ring in the middle of the blossom. The style (the part of the pistil bearing the stigma) is long, curved, and recurved.

LEAVES AND STEM:

The two- to six-foot stem is (usually) unbranched, ridged, and hairy, with alternate lanceolate to ovate, toothed leaves that are three to six inches long.

BLOOM SEASON:

June to September

Despite its common name (and genus name *Campanula*, Latin for "bell"), and unlike other members of the Bellflower family, including Southern Harebell (*Campanula divaricata;* see page 236), the five lobes of Tall Bellflower's blossoms are flat, creating a star shape rather than a bell. One of its most distinguishing features is the long style that extends far out from the petals and is twice curved, calling to mind the shape of old-fashioned drinking ladles.

The plant is far-ranging for, in addition to growing throughout the Blue Ridge and Great Smoky Mountains, it may be found from Ontario, Canada, to Florida, and as far west as Minnesota and South Dakota. Arranged in slender clusters along the upper portion of the two- to six-foot stem, the light blue to violet flowers contrast with the greenery of nearby vegetation in rich deciduous forests and moist clearings and thickets.

The Mesquakie Indians brewed a tea from the leaves to soothe coughs and treat tuberculosis. A concoction made by crushing the roots was thought to help those suffering from whooping cough.

When looking to other sources for information on Tall Bellflower, also known as American Bellflower, you should be aware that some reference books list it as *Campanulastrum americanum*.

Some places you may encounter Tall Bellflower include: lower elevations of GSMNP; BRP mileposts 81.9, 305, 370–375, 440.8, and 460.8; and along the dirt road portion of Haymakertown Road (VA 600) in Botetourt County, and Big House Mountain Trail near Lexington, Virginia.

VIPER'S BUGLOSS

Echium vulgare

The showy, bluish flowers are about an inch long and have noticeably protruding red stamens and an upper lip that is longer than the lower one.

The alternate, two- to six-inch, lanceolate leaves are sessile on the stem; the plant usually rises one to three feet from the ground.

June to September

It is believed that Viper's Bugloss was imported from Europe in the late 1600s; it has now become widespread and may be found along roadways and in meadows and other open areas throughout the Blue Ridge and Great Smoky Mountains.

You will be treated to a colorful display if you have a place where you can watch this plant grow from a young shoot to full blossom. Characteristic of the Forget-me-not family, of which Viper's Bugloss is a member, the plant's flowers are arranged in a one-sided coil that gradually unfolds as it grows. When they first appear, the buds are often a pleasing shade of pink. Spreading outward, the petals become a vivid purplish-blue, accented by long stamens of a rich red hue. Changing color again, the petals may become reddish-purple with age.

It received the first part of its common name because some people imagined its seed to look like the head of a snake. Some sources say it was given the name because the plant was believed to be a remedy for snakebites. The "bugloss" part of the name is from the Greek word for "ox-tongue," which the leaves supposedly resemble.

Be careful if you handle the plant because the tiny hairs on the leaves and along the stem have been known to cause an allergic reaction in some people.

Some places you may encounter Viper's Bugloss include: BRP mileposts 5–40; on the AT near Doll Flats along the North Carolina–Tennessee border, Pig Farm Campsite, Tar Jacket Ridge, and Humpback Mountain in central Virginia, and between Pine Grove Furnace State Park and PA 94 in Pennsylvania; and occasionally along the roadways of Catoctin Mountain Park in Maryland.

ASIATIC DAYFLOWER

Commelina communis

The half-inch-wide flowers have three green sepals and two rounded blue petals growing above a smaller white petal. There are three short stamens and three long ones.

The three- to five-inch, lanceolate leaves clasp the stem.

June to October

Considered by some people to be a bothersome weed, Asiatic Dayflower, also known as Common Dayflower, was imported from Asia and has escaped into the wild; it now has a range that stretches from Massachusetts to Alabama and as far west as Wisconsin and Kansas. In common with other members of the Spiderwort family, its small flowers last but a day.

While looking closely at the two upper, tiny, rounded flower petals, imagine ears and you will see why some people call the plant Mouse Flower. The species name *communis* refers to how the plant sometimes forms colonies, or communities, by taking root from its reclining stems.

Linnaeus named the flower *Commelina* for three Dutch brothers whose family name was Commelin. Two of the brothers were well known for their contributions to the field of botany, while the third died before he had a chance to make a reputation. Linnaeus saw a similarity with the Dayflower—the two upper petals being large and more prominent, and the lower petal smaller and less noticeable.

Also found in the area, the Virginia Dayflower (*Commelina virginica*) has an erect stem and three petals of equal size, all of which are blue. Slender Dayflower (*Commelina erecta*) has a more upright stem and white hairs around the leaves.

Some places you may encounter Asiatic Dayflower include: East Fifth Avenue in Rome, Georgia; BRP mileposts 232.5, 240.9, 373.9, and 467.8; on the AT between VA 311 and McAfee Knob in central Virginia; and west of the South River Bridge on the Chessie Nature Trail in Rockbridge County, and in Ivy Creek Natural Area near Charlottesville, Virginia.

CHICORY

Cichorium intybus

There are some plants that humans have yet to use, while there are others that we have adapted to multiple uses. Chicory is one of the latter.

The ancient Egyptians harvested the plant from gardens along the Nile River more than 5,000 years ago, and Christ's Greek contemporaries used it for medicinal purposes. The early colonists imported Chicory from the Old World, where it had been cultivated as livestock feed for centuries. Chicory's leaves have been added to salads, while its roots are dried and roasted to be used as a substitute for, or an additive to, coffee. You will find an abundance of references to people enjoying Chicory coffee, but it is certainly an acquired taste. The beverage is much stronger and quite a bit more bitter than the coffee most of us drink.

Dr. James A. Duke, author of *The Green Pharmacy,* suggests drinking two to four cups of Chicory coffee each day to keep the liver healthy, while recent scientific investigations have found that the plant has antibacterial properties and that a substance in its roots can lower heart rates.

Other common names include Bunk, Blue Sailors, and Wild Succory. The species name *intybus* comes from the Latin for "lettuce" or "greens," and refers to the way the leaves resemble endive.

Some places you may encounter Chicory include: BRP mileposts 115, 129–130, and 281.5; on the AT along VA 634 in southwest Virginia, and near the road crossing of VA 42 in central Virginia; Craig Creek Road (VA 779) in Craig County, and on the Lake Trail at Lake Robertson and Chessie Nature Trail near Lexington, Virginia; and along the C&O Canal Towpath in Maryland.

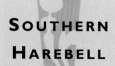

SOUTHERN
HAREBELL

Campanula divaricata

Arranged along slender stalks from which they nod, the bell-shaped flowers have five lobes that curve backward, five stamens, and a single long pistil.

Toothed and lanceolate to narrowly ovate, the one- to three-inch leaves are arranged alternately on the many-branched stem that grows from one to three feet high.

July to October

Southern Harebell favors rocky slopes, roadsides, and open woodlands. Not much more than a quarter inch in size, the blossoms can't help but bring a smile to your face when you spot their multitudes lining pathways winding through the mid-elevations of the Blue Ridge and Great Smoky Mountains. Bobbing up and down in response to hillside breezes, they're almost expected to tinkle, because the single, protruding pistil with a pale yellow tip so resembles a miniature clapper.

A variety of stories try to explain why the blossom is called Harebell. One says that it was once called Heatherbell, which became contracted to Hea'erbell, and eventually to Harebell. Another claims the plant was named for the hares that use its foliage to hide from predators, while a third explanation states that the name comes from the plant's hairy stems.

At one time, these beautiful blue flowers were referred to as Witch's Thimbles because of the Scottish belief that witches could transmogrify into hares. Other common names include Panicled Bellflower, Lady's Thimble, and Bluebell.

Tall Bellflower (*Campanula americana;* see page 228) is native to the area, but Creeping Bellflower (*Campanula rapunculoides*) is a European import that has escaped gardens and established itself in the wild. A Brothers Grimm fairy tale says that Rapunzel was named for this species because her father had to give her up in order to save his life after he was caught stealing the plant from a witch's garden.

Some places you may encounter Southern Harebell include: Schoolhouse Gap Trail, and Heintooga Ridge and Balsam Mountain Roads in GSMNP; and BRP mileposts 154.1, 162.4, 168, 208.5, 232.5, 235, 289.6, 305, 370–375, and 457.9.

GREAT LOBELIA

Lobelia siphilitica

The brilliant blue (occasionally pink or white) flowers grow from the axils of upper leaf bracts, are about an inch long, and have five petals that form two lips; the upper one has two lobes while the lower one has three spreading lobes marked with white. The five stamens are united in a tube around the single pistil.

The two- to six-inch, sessile leaves are lance- to egg-shaped and may be irregularly toothed or untoothed. They grow alternately on the smooth, two- to four-foot stem.

August to September

If you enjoy the beauty of the Cardinal Flower (*Lobelia cardinalis;* see page 198), be sure to seek out its relative, Great Lobelia, which has flower shapes and a stature very similar to the Cardinal Flower. Diana Wells, in her book *100 Flowers and How They Got Their Names,* says of both flowers, "They are a clear patriotic red and blue respectively." With their tubular shapes, both attract the same pollinators, including bees and hummingbirds.

Great Lobelia is not as common as Cardinal Flower. However, where you find one plant you will usually find a fairly good-sized colony. This is because, in addition to producing a large number of seeds, its stems form offshoots from the base, which send up new stems that produce more flowers and seeds the next growing season.

In the 1700s, Pehr Kalm, who is honored by the genus name for Mountain Laurel (*Kalmia latifolia;* see page 174), sent a report back to Europe that Native Americans used Great Lobelia as a cure for syphilis (thus, the species name *siphilitica*). Unfortunately, the treatment does not work and people who thought they were cured continued to spread the disease.

Native American tribes of the Midwest also believed that the plant had the ability to help reunite estranged lovers. Friends would chop up the root and place it into the couple's food without their knowledge. Of course, no one can say whether this works. What is known for sure is that the root contains alkaloids that may induce vomiting.

Some places you may encounter Great Lobelia include: Cades Cove, Oconaluftee Visitor Center, and other lower elevations in GSMNP; Oconaluftee Village Cherokee Botanical Garden Nature Trail in Cherokee, North Carolina; Southwest Virginia Agricultural Research and Extension Center off Hillman Highway between Glade Spring and Emory, Virginia; and BRP milepost 458.9.

239

MONKSHOOD

Aconitum uncinatum

The Monkshood has one of the most eccentric shapes of any flower. Of five irregular, petal-like sepals, the upper one forms a conspicuously rounded hood. This hood almost covers and hides two of the five small petals.

The three- to five-lobed leaves are roughly toothed. Sometimes unable to hold the weight of its leaves and flowers, the two- to four-foot stem is often found leaning on other plants.

August to October

Like other flowers, Monkshood has a shape designed to insure pollination. The lower sepals serve as a landing pad for visiting insects, while other sepals close in to guide the visitors and make certain that they brush against the stamens and pistils on their way to the two petals that hold the nectar deep inside the hood.

It is believed that the genus name *Aconitum* comes from the word *akone,* which means "rocky" or "cliff," because Monkshood and other members of the genus grow in such environments. Other sources claim that the word is derived from a word that means "dagger" or "arrow," and refers to the practice of ancient warriors' dipping their weapons into a solution made from the highly poisonous plants.

Linnaeus reported that the plants are fatal to grazing cattle and goats, and researchers have observed field mice avoiding the plants, even during hard times when food is scarce. A story in Greek mythology says the plants became poisonous when drool from the mouth of Cerberus, the keeper of the gates of hell, dropped onto the plant as Hercules dragged him from Hades.

Despite its toxic nature (as little as a teaspoon of the root can paralyze the heart or respiratory system), homeopathic practitioners have prescribed aconite (the substance obtained from the plants) for a variety of symptoms from earaches to cold feet to infectious diseases. Commission E, the German group that is gradually becoming recognized as the world's foremost experts on herbal remedies, specifically recommends staying away from any treatment involving aconite.

Some places you may encounter Monkshood include: Balsam Mountain Road, Mount LeConte, and The Boulevard Trail in GSMNP; and on the AT close to Roan Highlands Shelter along the North Carolina–Tennessee border, and Apple Orchard Mountain in central Virginia.

SOAPWORT
GENTIAN

Gentiana saponaria

Growing in terminal clusters and from the axils of upper leaves, the corollas of the one-inch flowers open slightly at the summit. The petals range from purplish-blue to lilac to white.

The leaves grow in pairs along a twelve- to thirty-inch stem.

September to October

If, as many people have likened them to, the lofty forests of the southern Appalachian Mountains are cathedrals, then the flowers of the Gentians are the churches' candles, their upright, tubular blossoms spreading a purplish-blue glow about the sanctuaries. Dozens of the flowers grow on each plant, which produce copious amounts of small seeds, enabling them to establish large colonies. One observer watched a species of Gentian go from several dozen plants to more than 1,000 in the space of ten years.

There are close to 75 genera and 1,000 species of Gentians found in a variety of environments in the subtropical and temperate regions of the world. Within the Blue Ridge and Great Smoky Mountains you may also find Bottle Gentian (*Gentiana andrewsii;* see page 255), whose deep blue petals stay completely closed. Stiff Gentian (*Gentiana quinquefolia*) has scores of the flowers growing on each plant, with a couple of observers saying they had counted more than 300 on a single plant. In addition to having so many individual flowers, the species may be distinguished from other Gentians by the smaller size and lighter purple color of its blossoms.

Gentians were used by Native Americans and early settlers as a tonic to help digestion and stimulate the appetite. Have you ever visited New England and drunk a locally produced soft drink called Moxie? If so, you have discovered the distinctive flavor of an extract of Gentian.

Some places you may encounter one of the Gentians include: East Fifth Avenue in Rome, Georgia; Heintooga Ridge Road in GSMNP; BRP mileposts 85.8, 363-368, 422.4, 431, and 451.2; and on the AT along the field edges of Cold Mountain and Tar Jacket Ridge in central Virginia.

GREEN TO BROWN FLOWERS

SKUNK CABBAGE
Symplocarpus foetidus

FLOWER:

The small flowers of this plant are borne on a rounded spadix sheathed by an enveloping mottled spathe that ranges in color from green to dirty purple.

LEAVES AND STEM:

The veined leaves are heart-shaped at the base and resemble cabbage leaves. Having been tightly wrapped, they unfurl after the flower has bloomed.

BLOOM SEASON:

February to April (may bloom even earlier in some years)

Because it sometimes blooms while there is still snow on the ground, Skunk Cabbage has developed a mechanism to withstand the cold. By burning carbohydrates stored in its large root system and produced from the cellular respiration resulting from its rapid growth, it is capable of producing its own heat—often melting the snow and ice around it. Temperatures inside its spathe have been found to be as much as twenty-seven degrees higher than the surrounding air.

Once the flower fades away, cabbage-like leaves that can be up to three feet long and one foot wide grow on stalks that can reach a height of two feet. In some moist areas—their preferred habitat—they can become the dominant foliage. When young, the leaves are edible if boiled through several changes of water to remove the fetid odor and taste, and were once used to relieve the pains of rheumatism.

The roots contain calcium oxalate crystals, making them taste hot when eaten; they are somewhat poisonous when uncooked. Despite this, the plant was listed in the *United States Pharmacopeia* for more than sixty years in the 1800s with instructions to use it for the treatment of epilepsy, coughs, trismus, and asthma.

The genus name *Symplocarpus* is derived from two Greek words, *symploke* and *karpos,* which translates into "connected fruit" and refers to how the ovaries of the fruiting stalk grow together. The species name *foetidus* obviously means "fetid" or "foul odor."

Some places you may encounter Skunk Cabbage include: BRP mileposts 176.1, 185.8, and 217; on the AT near Fuller Lake in Pine Grove Furnace State Park in Pennsylvania; along the trails of Sky Meadows State Park in Virginia; near the beginning of the Old Rag Trail in SNP; and in the lower elevations of Catoctin Mountain Park in Maryland.

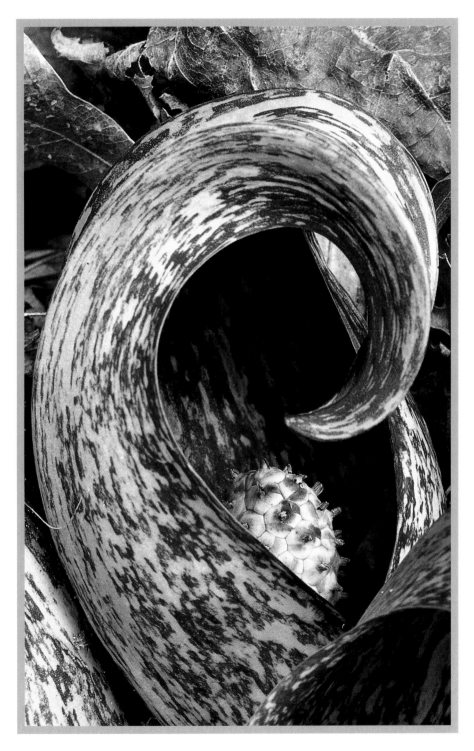

245

WILD GINGER

Asarum canadense

Ha, ha, ha. You and me. Little brown jug, how I love thee.

Sure, this song was written about some fellow's predilection for liquor, but it could easily be the recitation of the small gnats that crawl into Wild Ginger's little brown jug-shaped flowers to feast on the abundant pollen, escape chilly breezes, and lay eggs.

But just as liquor can become a curse for those who enjoy it, Wild Ginger also exacts a price. The plant's tissue contains a poison that kills the gnat larvae as they feed, permitting the seeds to grow to maturity without being eaten. Once they get big enough, their leathery container breaks open, spilling them onto the ground. Like those of the Sharp-Lobed Hepatica (*Hepatica acutiloba;* see page 150), the seeds may end up being dispersed by ants who are attracted to, and eat, the nodules (known as elaiosomes) that are attached to the seeds' outer walls.

The word ginger is derived from the Sanskrit *srngaverem,* which translates as "body with horns," a phrase that certainly describes the flower's pointed lobes. Wild Ginger root has been substituted for the ginger often called for in Asian food recipes but has also been used for a variety of medicinal purposes. A tea made from the root was drunk to treat whooping cough, stomach cramps, and colic, and was used as an appetite stimulant. However, be warned that recent studies show that the plant contains an acid that may cause cancer.

Some places you may encounter Wild Ginger include: Sosebee Cove in Union County, and Amicalola Falls and Tallulah Gorge State Parks in Georgia; Little River and Cooper Road Trails, and Newfound Gap Road in GSMNP; on the AT between Jennings Creek to north of Bryant Ridge Shelter in central Virginia, and in Caledonia State Park in Pennsylvania; and in the lowlands of Catoctin Mountain Park in Maryland.

247

JACK-IN-THE-PULPIT

Arisaema triphyllum

The actual flower is hard to find. It is at the bottom of the spadix ("Jack"), which is hidden by the flaplike spathe.

There are usually two leaves, divided into three or five segments, rising from the base of the plant and growing one to three feet in height.

April to late June

Many people think that the green, white, or purple sheath with a hood—the "pulpit"—that surrounds and covers "Jack" is the plant's flower. Actually, the sheath is just a leaf bract; in order to see the diminutive flowers, you need to lift the hood and look inside: they are clustered around Jack's base. Interestingly, the sheath is often pale green in woods that receive a large amount of sunlight, while plants that grow in deeply shaded areas are, as a general rule, a deep purple. Later in the summer, the "pulpit" falls away to reveal the red berries that have developed from the flowers.

The Jack-in-the-Pulpit is not a plant that eats insects, but those that crawl to the bottom of the pouch in search of pollen often cannot escape. The sides of the wall are slippery, while an overhanging ledge prevents climbing up the spadix. Some creatures may find a tiny hole where the two sides of the spathe come together, but many insects are too large or not strong enough to push through. As a result, many die inside the plant, causing some botanists to speculate that the Jack-in-the-Pulpit is gradually evolving into an insectivorous plant.

The species name *triphyllum* refers to the plants' leaves, usually divided into three segments.

Some places you may encounter Jack-in-the-Pulpit include: Joyce Kilmer Memorial Forest in North Carolina; Tremont Road, and Smokemount Nature and Huskey Gap Trails in GSMNP; BRP mileposts 85, 294, and 308.2; on the AT on Springer Mountain in Georgia, Pearis Mountain in southwest Virginia, Sawtooth Ridge in central Virginia, and between Gravel Springs Gap and Thornton Gap in SNP; Dragon's Tooth Trail in Craig County, Freer Trail in Blackwater Creek Natural Area in Lynchburg, Crabtree Falls Trail in Nelson County, and North Ridge Trail in Sky Meadows State Park, Virginia; and Gambrill State Park, and Deerfield Nature Trail in Catoctin Mountain Park in Maryland.

FALSE HELLEBORE

Veratrum viride

FLOWER:
False Hellebore's half-inch, star-shaped, greenish, hairy flowers grow in packed clusters at the top of the stem.

LEAVES AND STEM:
The broadly oval, heavily ribbed leaves are six to twelve inches long and three to six inches wide, and are sessile with a clasping base.

BLOOM SEASON:
May to July

False Hellebore is known by a variety of common names including American White Hellebore, Swamp Hellebore, Pokeroot, and Itchweed. The latter is obviously an admonition not to touch the plant—some people have had severe allergic reactions, and "Itchweed" is a subdued warning, considering how dangerous the plant can be.

People who called it Big-Bane or Devil's Bite must have learned the hard way that its foliage and rootstock have proven fatal to grazing animals as well as humans who have mistaken it for an edible plant. Symptoms of acute poisoning include vomiting, diarrhea, stomach cramps, spasms, paralysis, difficulty breathing, headaches, and excessive salivation. In addition, hallucinations may happen and the heart rate become so depressed that death occurs. One of its other common names, Indian Poke, refers to the story that says some chiefs of Native American tribes were permitted to ascend to that position only after they had survived eating the plant.

Because they both enjoy moist environments, the Skunk Cabbage (*Symplocarpus foetidus;* see page 244) and the False Hellebore are often found growing side by side. Small-flowered False Hellebore (*Veratrum parviflorum*) may be found in drier environments and is a shorter plant whose leaves are stalked and almost entirely basal.

Some places you may encounter False Hellebore include: Mount Mitchell State Park, Yellow Mountain Trail in Jackson County, and Green Ridge Trail in Madison County, North Carolina; on Heintooga Ridge Road and Gregory Bald Trail in GSMNP; BRP mileposts 364.6 and 425.5; on the AT on Bryant Ridge in central Virginia and between Big Meadows and Fishers Gap Overlook in SNP; and south of Pine Swamp Road on Big Savage Hiking Trail in Garrett County, and in the lowlands of Catoctin Mountain Park in Maryland.

RELATED OR SIMILAR SPECIES

SPOTTED JEWELWEED
Impatiens capensis See page 124

PURPLE TRILLIUM
Trillium erectum See page 30

LARGE-FLOWERED TRILLIUM
Trillium grandiflorum See page 30

SWEET WHITE TRILLIUM
Trillium simile See page 30

PAINTED TRILLIUM
Trillium undulatum See page 30

VASEY'S TRILLIUM
Trillium vaseyi See page 30

WHITE CAMPION
Silene latifolia See page 42

CATAWBA RHODODENDRON
Rhododendron catawbiensis See page 64

ONE-FLOWERED CANCER ROOT
Orobanche uniflora See page 108

PINK LADY'S SLIPPER
Cypripedium acaule See page 112

GRAY'S LILY
Lilium grayi See page 138

LARGE PURPLE-FRINGED ORCHID
Habenaria grandiflora See page 142

TALL GOLDENROD
Solidago altissima See page 136

ROUND-LOBED HEPATICA
Hepatica americana See page 150

BOTTLE GENTIAN
Gentiana andrewsii See page 242

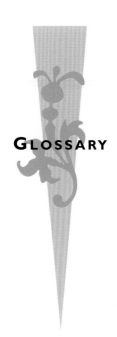

Glossary

ANTHER: The part of the stamen containing the pollen.

AXIL: The (upper) point where the leaf and the stem meet.

BASAL: At the bottom of the stem.

BRACT: A modified leaf (that may be green or colored) growing near or below a flower.

CALYX: A term that collectively takes in the outer sepals.

COMPOUND: Divided into separate parts.

CORM: A bulblike underground part of a plant stem where food is stored.

COROLLA: A term that takes in all of the petals of the flower.

DISK: The numerous, tiny tube flowers that are found in the center of a flower head or that make up the entire head in some flowers.

DOCTRINE OF SIGNATURES: The belief that whatever a plant looks like it can cure. For example, it is believed that members of the Snapdragon family are useful in treating throat sicknesses because of the mouth-and-throat form of the blossoms.

LANCEOLATE: Longer than it is broad, like the blade of a lance or spear.

OVATE: Shaped like an egg, with the base being wider than the tip.

PETAL: One of the separate divisions of the corolla; a distinct part of the flower that is often brightly colored.

PINNATE: A compound leaf whose leaflets are arranged along the main stalk (think of the way a feather is arranged).

PISTIL: A flower's female organ.

RACEME: A long stalk from which emanate a number of flowers growing on their own stems.

RHIZOME: A (usually) horizontal underground stem that has food stored in nodes and that sends up shoots.

ROSETTE: Refers to leaves that grow in a circle around the base of a stem.

SEPAL: A modified leaf that surrounds the reproductive organs; collectively known as the calyx.

SESSILE: Having no stalk.

SPADIX: A thick stem on which many small flowers are crowded.

SPATHE: A leaf bract (or bracts) that enfolds or forms a hood around a spadix.

STAMEN: A flower's male organ.

STIGMA: The tip of the pistil, which receives the pollen.

STIPULE: The tiny leaflike appendage (usually growing in pairs) at the base of the leaf stalk.

STYLE: The part of the pistil bearing the stigma.

TEPAL: A sepal that resembles a petal.

TERMINAL: Growing at the tip of the stem.

UMBEL: A flower cluster in which all flower stalks grow from the same point.

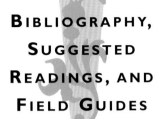

Adams, Kevin, and Marty Casstevens. *Wildflowers of the Southern Appalachians: How to Photograph and Identify Them.* Winston-Salem, N.C.: John F. Blair, 1996.

Adkins, Leonard M. *The Appalachian Trail: A Visitor's Companion.* Birmingham, Ala.: Menasha Ridge Press, 1998.

—————— *Fifty Hikes in Maryland: Walks, Hikes, and Backpacks from the Allegheny Plateau to the Atlantic Ocean.* Woodstock, Vt.: Backcountry Guides, 2000.

—————— *Fifty Hikes in Northern Virginia: Walks, Hikes, and Backpacks from the Allegheny Mountains to the Chesapeake Bay.* Woodstock, Vt.: Backcountry Guides, 2000.

—————— *Fifty Hikes in Southern Virginia: From the Cumberland Gap to the Atlantic Ocean.* Woodstock, Vt.: Backcountry Guides, 2002.

—————— *Maryland: An Explorer's Guide.* Woodstock, Vt.: Countryman Press, 2002.

—————— *Walking the Blue Ridge: A Guide to the Trails of the Blue Ridge Parkway.* Chapel Hill: University of North Carolina Press, 2003.

—————— *Wildflowers of the Appalachian Trail.* Birmingham, Ala.: Menasha Ridge Press, 1999.

Alderman, J. Anthony. *Wildflowers of the Blue Ridge Parkway.* Chapel Hill, N.C.: University of North Carolina Press, 1997.

Appalachian Trail Guides (a series of books available from the Appalachian Trail Conference, Harpers Ferry, W.V.).

Barnette, Martha. *A Garden of Words.* New York: Times Books, 1992.

Bartram, William. *Travels.* Salt Lake City: Peregrine Smith, 1980.

Borland, Hal. *A Countryman's Flowers.* New York: Alfred A. Knopf, 1981.

Bull, John, and John Farrand, Jr. *National Audubon Society Field Guide to Birds: Eastern Region.* New York: Alfred A. Knopf, 1997.

Burns, Barbara. *North American Wildflowers.* New York: Gramercy Books, 1992.

Busch, Phyllis S. *Wildflowers and the Stories behind Their Names.* New York: Charles Scribner's Sons, 1977.

Castleman, Michael. *The New Healing Herbs: The Ultimate Guide to Nature's Best Medicines.* New York: Bantam Books, 2002.

Coats, Alice. *Flowers and Their Histories.* New York: McGraw Hill, 1971.

Dietz, Marjorie J. *The Concise Encyclopedia of Favorite Wild Flowers.* Garden City, N.Y.: 1965.

Duke, James A. *The Green Pharmacy.* New York: St. Martin's, 1998.

Durant, Mary. *Who Named the Daisy? Who Named the Rose?* New York: Dodd, Mead, 1976.

Eastman, John. *Forest and Thicket: Trees, Shrubs, and Wildflowers of Eastern North America.* Mechanicsburg, Pa.: Stackpole Books, 1992.

Gerarde, John. *Herball.* New York: D.K., 1984.

Gibbons, Euell. *Stalking the Wild Asparagus.* Chambersburg, Pa.: Alan C. Hood, 1987.

Gray, Asa. *Manual of Botany.* New York: American Book, 1908.

Grimm, William Carey. *The Illustrated Book of Wildflowers and Shrubs: The Comprehensive Field Guide to More than 1,300 Plants of Eastern North America.* Mechanicsburg, Pa.: Stackpole Books, 1993.

BIBLIOGRAPHY, SUGGESTED READINGS, AND FIELD GUIDES

Gupton, Oscar W., and Fred C. Swope. *Wildflowers of the Shenandoah Valley and Blue Ridge Mountains.* Charlottesville: University of Virginia Press, 1993.

Hatfield, Audrey Wynne. *Pleasures of Wild Plants.* New York: Tangier, 1966.

Hedrick, U. P., editor. *Sturtevant's Edible Plants of the World.* New York: Dover, 1972.

Hersey, Jean. *The Woman's Day Book of Wildflowers.* New York: Simon and Schuster, 1976.

Hill, Sir John. *The Family Herbal.* Bungoy, England: Brightly and Kinnersley, 1800.

Hutson, Robert W., William F. Hutson, and Aaron J. Sharp. *Great Smoky Mountains Wildflowers.* Northbrook, Ill.: Windy Pines, 1995.

Hylander, Clarence J. *Flowers of the Field and Forest.* New York: Macmillan, 1962.

Klimas, John E., and James A. Cunningham. *Wildflowers of Eastern America.* New York: Alfred A. Knopf, 1974.

Little, Herbert L. *National Audubon Society Field Guide to North American Trees: Eastern Region.* New York: Alfred A. Knopf, 1994.

Martin, Laura C. *Garden Flower Folklore.* Old Saybrook, Conn.: Globe Pequot, 1987.

_____ *Southern Wildflowers.* Marietta, Ga.: Longstreet, 1989.

_____ *Wildflower Folklore.* Old Saybrook, Conn.: Globe Pequot, 1993.

Niering, William A., Nancy C. Olmstead, and John W. Thieret. *National Audubon Society Field Guide to North American Flowers: Eastern Region.* New York: Alfred A. Knopf, 2001.

Peterson, Roger Tory, and Margeret McKenny. *A Field Guide to Wildflowers: Northeastern/North-central North America.* Boston: Houghton Mifflin, 1996.

Rickett, H. W. *The Odyssey Book of American Wildflowers.* New York: Odyssey, 1964.

Russell, Sharman Apt. *Anatomy of a Rose: Exploring the Secret Life of Flowers.* Cambridge, Mass.: Perseus, 2001.

Sanders, Jack. *Hedgemaids and Fairy Candles: The Lives and Lore of North American Wildflowers.* Camden, Me.: Ragged Mountain, 1993.

Schaeffer, Elizabeth. *Dandelion, Pokeweed, and Goosefoot: How the Early Settlers Used Plants for Food, Medicine, and in the Home.* Reading, Mass.: Addison Wesley, 1972.

Silverman, Maida. *A City Herbal.* New York: Alfred A. Knopf, 1997.

Smith, Richard M. *Wildflowers of the Southern Mountains.* Knoxville: The University of Tennessee Press, 1998.

Stokes, Donald W. *The Natural History of Wild Shrubs and Vines: Eastern and Central North America.* New York: Harper and Row, 1981.

Wells, Diana. *100 Flowers and How They Got Their Names.* Chapel Hill, N.C.: Algonquin Books, 1997.

White, Peter, et al. *Wildflowers of the Smokies.* Gatlinburg, Tenn.: Great Smoky Mountains Natural History Association,

A number of organizations and groups work hard to preserve and protect the Blue Ridge and Great Smoky Mountains from the encroachments and destructions of the modern world. Among those that deserve your support are:

FRIENDS OF GREAT SMOKY MOUNTAINS NATIONAL PARK
107 Joy Street
Sevierville, TN 37864-5650
(800) 845-5665

160 South Main Street
Waynesville, NC 28786
(828) 452-0720; www.friendsofthesmokies.org

GREAT SMOKY MOUNTAINS ASSOCIATION
115 Park Headquarters Road
Gatlinburg, TN 37738
(888) 898-9102; www.smokiesstore.org

FRIENDS OF THE BLUE RIDGE PARKWAY
P. O. Box 341
Arden, NC 28704
(704) 687-8722

P. O. Box 20986
Roanoke, VA 24018
(800) 228-7275; www.blueridgefriends.org

BLUE RIDGE PARKWAY FOUNDATION
P. O. Box 10247 Salem Station
Winston-Salem, NC 27108-0427
(336) 721-0260; www.brpfoundation.org

APPALACHIAN TRAIL CONFERENCE
P. O. Box 807
Harpers Ferry, WV 25425-0807
(304) 535-6331; www.atconf.org

FRIENDS OF SHENANDOAH NATIONAL PARK
Route 4 Box 248
Luray, VA 22835
(202) 387-9128 or (540) 999-3500

SHENANDOAH NATIONAL PARK ASSOCIATION
3655 US Highway 211 East
Luray, VA 22835
(540) 999-3582; www.snpbooks.org

APPALACHIAN VOICES
703 West King Street, Suite 105
Boone, NC 28607
(828) 262-1500; www.appvoices.org

The meetings and outings of local native-plant societies are excellent places to learn more about wildflowers and make friends with people who share your interest.

ORGANIZATIONS

GEORGIA NATIVE PLANT SOCIETY
P. O. Box 422085
Atlanta, GA 30342-2085
(770) 343-6000; www.gnps.org

TENNESSEE NATIVE PLANT SOCIETY
c/o Department of Botany
University of Tennessee
Knoxville, TN 37996

NORTH CAROLINA WILDFLOWER PRESERVATION SOCIETY
North Carolina Botanical Gardens
Totten Garden Center 3375
University of North Carolina
Chapel Hill, NC 27599-3375
www.ncwildflower.org

VIRGINIA NATIVE PLANT SOCIETY
400 Blandy Farm Lane, Unit 2
Boyce, VA 22610
(540) 837-1600; www.vnps.org

MARYLAND NATIVE PLANT SOCIETY
P. O. Box 4877
Silver Spring, MD 20914
www.mdflora.org

PENNSYLVANIA NATIVE PLANT SOCIETY
P. O. Box 281
State College, PA 19087
www.pawildflower.org

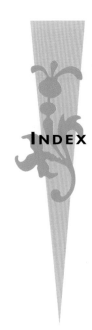

INDEX

263